America's Best-Loved
Community Cookbook
Recipes

Desserts

Better Homes and Gardens.

Better Homes and Gardens® Books
Des Moines

Better Homes and Gardens® Books
An Imprint of Meredith® Books

America's Best-Loved Community Cookbook Recipes
Desserts
Editor: Christopher Cavanaugh
Associate Art Director: Lynda Haupert
Designer: Jeff Harrison
Copywriter: Kim Gayton Elliott
Copyeditor: Kathy Roberts
Production Manager: Doug Johnston

Editor-in-Chief: James D. Blume
Director, New Product Development: Ray Wolf
Test Kitchen Director: Sharon Stilwell

Better Homes and Gardens® Magazine
Editor-in-Chief: Jean LemMon
Executive Food Editor: Nancy Byal

Meredith Publishing Group
President, Publishing Group: Christopher M. Little
Vice President and Publishing Director: John P. Loughlin

Meredith Corporation
Chairman and Chief Executive Officer: Jack D. Rehm
President and Chief Operating Officer: William T. Kerr

Chairman of the Executive Committee: E.T. Meredith III

On the cover: Lemon Luscious Pie (see recipe, page 67)

Our seal assures you that every recipe in **America's Best-Loved Community Cookbook Recipes** *Desserts* has been tested in the *Better Homes and Gardens® Test Kitchen.* This means that each recipe is practical and reliable, and meets our high standards of taste appeal. We guarantee your satisfaction with this book for as long as you own it.

desserts

Americans love dessert. It provides the grand finale to many a memorable meal—and causes many a mouthwatering fantasy. From the surprisingly wholesome to the divinely decadent, this collection proves that communities across the country enjoy their sweets in high style.

Cakes, cookies, candies, pies, and puddings are all represented in this fifth volume of Better Homes and Gardens® *America's Best-Loved Community Cookbook Recipes: Desserts.* These cherished delicacies include such regional specialties as Texas Sheet Cake and Georgia's Pecan Pie, and traditions from other lands such as Swedish Jul Grot and Spanish-inspired Oat and Banana Cookies. Some are just phenomenal creations, such as the strawberries-and-cream Blitz Torte, Peanut Butter Pie, and minty Grasshopper Bars. You'll find enough concoctions to drive a chocolate lover to distraction, including gooey Mississippi Mud, creamy Chocolate Chess Pie, and Ultimate Hunka Chocolate Cookies. Fruit lovers are blessed with Old-Fashioned Strawberry Shortcake, Ronnie's Mom's Apple Dumplings, and Ruby Date Bars. And, naturally, each recipe has been awarded the *Better Homes and Gardens® Test Kitchen* seal of approval, so you know you can trust these recipes.

Plus, the *Better Homes and Gardens® Test Kitchen* has added tips on how to make the flakiest pastry crust, quick-and-easy ways to chop chocolate, and methods for cutting perfectly square bar cookies. And there's so much more. Take a look—these miraculous dishes are sure to send you into a reverie of dessert making. Sweet dreams!

contents

cakes

The answer to a dessert lover's fantasy, this chapter is overflowing with the most sublime assortment of dreamy cakes. Enchant your family with a homespun classic, such as Applesauce Cake or Old-Fashioned Strawberry Shortcake. Bewitch your friends with Cheesecake Squares or a traditional Black Forest Cake. Need an enthralling finish when feeding a crowd? Texas Sheet Cake will dazzle the hungriest hoard. Want to charm the chocoholics in your crowd? That Chocolate Thing, Mississippi Mud, or decadent Chocolate Cheesecake will satiate even the most ardent cocoa lover. Pick a cake, any cake—each is a dream come true.

THAT CHOCOLATE THING

THAT CHOCOLATE THING

Makes 16 to 20 Servings
- 1 pound semisweet chocolate, cut up
- 1 pound butter (2 cups)
- 1 cup sugar
- 6 eggs
- 2 tablespoons all-purpose flour
- ⅓ cup water
- ½ cup sliced almonds

Fresh raspberries *or* fresh strawberries, sliced (optional)

Whipped cream

◆　◆　◆

When the taste-testing committee for Peninsula Potpourri *sampled Ursula Spector's That Chocolate Thing, the rich, chocolaty dessert was a big hit with everyone—including a local food editor. Although Ursula usually saves the mouth-watering dessert for company, her family loves it, too. She warns, however, that you may want to serve That Chocolate Thing following a light meal.*

Ursula Spector
Peninsula Potpourri
The Children's Health Council
Palo Alto
CALIFORNIA

1 Preheat the oven to 300°. Line a 9-inch springform pan with foil and then brush with butter; set aside.

2 In a 2- or 3-quart saucepan, cook the chocolate, butter and sugar over low heat, stirring constantly until the chocolate and butter are melted. Remove from heat and cool.

3 Beat the eggs just until they are blended.

4 In a small bowl, stir together the flour and water until smooth. Add the eggs and flour mixture to the chocolate mixture; stir until smooth. Pour the batter into the prepared pan. Sprinkle the top with the almonds.

5 Place the batter-filled springform pan in a baking pan on an oven rack. Pour *water* into the baking pan around the springform pan to a depth of ½ inch.

6 Bake in the 300° oven about 2½ hours or until the dessert is evenly puffed and a wooden toothpick inserted near the center comes out clean. Cool in the pan. The dessert will fall evenly over its entire surface.

7 Cover and chill for 24 hours. Remove the dessert from the pan and peel off the foil. If desired, sprinkle with fresh raspberries or sliced strawberries. Serve thin slices with a dollop of whipped cream.

 TIPS FROM OUR KITCHEN

Sixteen ounces (2 cups) of semisweet chocolate pieces or sixteen 1-ounce squares of semisweet chocolate can be used for the chocolate in the recipe.

Do not substitute margarine for the butter in this recipe.

Lining the springform pan with foil keeps the batter from leaking during baking.

Nutrition Analysis (*Per Serving*): Calories: 460 / Cholesterol: 152 mg / Carbohydrates: 31 g / Protein: 6 g / Sodium: 263 mg / Fat: 39 g (Saturated Fat: 23 g) / Potassium: 179 mg.

BLACK FOREST CAKE

Makes 16 Servings

Fudge Cake:
- 1 cup margarine *or* butter, softened
- 2 cups sugar
- 4 eggs
- 2 cups all-purpose flour
- 1½ teaspoons baking soda
- ¼ teaspoon salt
- ⅔ cup buttermilk
- 1 teaspoon vanilla
- 3 squares (3-ounces) unsweetened chocolate, finely chopped

Cherry Filling:
- 1 16- *or* 17-ounce can pitted dark sweet cherries
- ¼ cup water
- 2 tablespoons cornstarch

Whipped Cream:
- 3 cups heavy whipping cream
- ¼ cup sifted powdered sugar
- 2 to 4 tablespoons kirsch (clear cherry brandy)

Chocolate-Buttercream Filling:
- ½ cup margarine *or* butter, softened
- 4 cups sifted powdered sugar
- 3 tablespoons heavy whipping cream
- 1 teaspoon vanilla
- 3 squares (3 ounces) semisweet chocolate, melted and cooled

For Assembly:
- 1 tablespoon kirsch
- ½ square (½ ounce) semisweet chocolate, grated *or* shaved

◆   ◆   ◆

Mrs. Hans Eckhardt
Furniture City Feasts
The Junior League of High Point
High Point
NORTH CAROLINA

1 Preheat the oven to 325°. Grease and flour three 9x1½-inch round baking pans. Set aside.

2 To make the Fudge Cake: In a large mixing bowl, cream the 1 cup margarine or butter and the sugar until fluffy. Add the eggs, one at a time, beating for 1 minute after each addition.

3 In a medium mixing bowl, stir together the flour, baking soda and salt. Add the flour mixture and buttermilk alternately to the creamed mixture. Beat in the 1 teaspoon vanilla.

4 Melt the 3 squares unsweetened chocolate in ⅔ cup *boiling water*, stirring until smooth. Blend the chocolate mixture into the batter.

5 Pour the batter into the prepared pans. Bake in the 325° oven for 30 to 35 minutes or until a wooden toothpick inserted in the center comes out clean. Cool the cake layers for 10 minutes in the pans; remove from the pans and cool on wire racks.

6 To make the Cherry Filling: Drain the cherries, reserving the syrup. In a small saucepan over medium heat, stir together the cherry syrup, water and cornstarch. Cook and stir until the mixture is thickened and bubbly. Cook and stir for 2 minutes more. Stir in the cherries. Set aside to cool.

7 To make the Whipped Cream: In a large bowl, whip the 3 cups whipping cream with the ¼ cup powdered sugar and the 2 to 4 tablespoons kirsch until stiff peaks form (tips stand straight). Set aside.

8 To make the Chocolate-Buttercream Filling: In a mixing bowl, cream the margarine or butter with the 4 cups powdered sugar. Beat in the 3 tablespoons whipping cream and the vanilla. Add the melted semisweet chocolate and continue to beat until smooth.

9 To assemble the cake: Place one cake layer on a serving plate. Using a pastry tube, pipe a ring of the Chocolate-Buttercream Filling around the edge of the layer. Place a second ring of Chocolate-Buttercream Filling 2 inches in from the first. Fill in the uncovered area with all of the Cherry Filling. Chill just until set.

10 Place a second cake layer on top of the first. Prick the top of this layer with a fork and sprinkle it with the 1 tablespoon kirsch. Spread with the remaining Chocolate-Buttercream Filling.

11 Place the third layer on top. Spread the top and sides of the entire cake with the Whipped Cream. Garnish with the grated or shaved chocolate. Refrigerate until serving time.

Nutrition Analysis (*Per Serving*): Calories: 569 / Cholesterol: 78 mg / Carbohydrates: 78 g / Protein: 5 g / Sodium: 350 mg / Fat: 29 g (Saturated Fat: 8 g) / Potassium: 189 mg.

BLACK FOREST CAKE

TEXAS SHEET CAKE

TEXAS SHEET CAKE

Makes 32 Servings
Cake:
2   cups all-purpose flour
2   cups granulated sugar
1   teaspoon baking soda
½   teaspoon salt
1   cup margarine *or* butter
1   cup water
¼   cup unsweetened cocoa
    powder
2   eggs
1   cup dairy sour cream
Frosting:
½   cup margarine *or* butter
⅓   cup milk
¼   cup unsweetened cocoa
    powder
4½ cups sifted powdered sugar
1   teaspoon vanilla

❖   ❖   ❖

Tobie Frank said that Texas Sheet Cake "is the moistest cake—and it lasts forever!" Tobie's friend shared the recipe with her about 15 years ago, and Tobie said she usually makes the sheet cake— her favorite basic chocolate cake recipe—when her children have their friends over to visit.

Tobie Frank
The Best of the Best
Rodef Shalom Sisterhood
Pittsburgh
PENNSYLVANIA

1 Preheat the oven to 350°. Grease and flour a 15x10x1-inch baking pan; set aside.

2 To make the cake: In a large mixing bowl, combine the flour, granulated sugar, baking soda and salt; set aside.

3 In a medium saucepan, stir together the 1 cup margarine or butter, the water and the ¼ cup cocoa powder. Bring the mixture just to a boil, stirring constantly; remove from heat.

4 Add the cocoa mixture to the flour mixture. Beat with an electric mixer on low speed until all of the ingredients are well blended. Add the eggs and sour cream. Beat on medium to high speed for 1 minute more.

   TIPS FROM OUR KITCHEN

The size of the pan is very important when you're baking cakes and bar cookies. If you don't have a 15x10x1-inch pan, use two 11x7½x1½-inch pans or two 9-inch square baking pans.

5 Pour the batter into the prepared baking pan. Bake in the 350° oven about 25 minutes or until a wooden toothpick inserted near the center of the cake comes out clean; remove from oven.

6 Meanwhile, to make the frosting: In a medium saucepan, stir together the ½ cup margarine or butter, the milk and the ¼ cup cocoa powder. Bring the mixture to a boil; remove from heat. Add the powdered sugar and vanilla. Beat with an electric mixer on medium speed until the frosting is smooth.

7 Pour the warm frosting over the warm sheet cake, spreading the frosting evenly. Let the cake cool in the pan on a wire rack.

You'll get better volume in the cake batter if all of the ingredients are at room temperature when you combine them. However, don't let the eggs or sour cream sit out for more than 30 minutes. Preheating the oven also helps the cake to rise properly.

Nutrition Analysis (*Per Serving*): Calories: 228 / Cholesterol: 16 mg / Carbohydrates: 33 g / Protein: 2 g / Sodium: 180 mg / Fat: 10 g (Saturated Fat: 2 g) / Potassium: 30 mg.

CHOCOLATE DEVIL'S FOOD CAKE

Makes 12 Servings

Cake:

1	cup granulated sugar
½	cup unsweetened cocoa powder
½	cup sour milk
1	cup granulated sugar
½	cup butter *or* margarine, softened
2	eggs
2	cups all-purpose flour
1	teaspoon baking soda
1	cup sour milk
1	teaspoon vanilla

Chocolate Glaze:

2	squares (2 ounces) semisweet chocolate, chopped
2	tablespoons butter *or* margarine
¾	cup sifted powdered sugar

◆   ◆   ◆

This decadent recipe for Chocolate Devil's Food Cake was submitted to the St. Thomas' Church cookbook by Mrs. W. G. Mayer, a parishioner's mother-in-law. Proceeds from cookbook sales are used to help feed the hungry and to aid in the upkeep of the historic church.

Mrs. W. G. Mayer
Two and Company
St. Thomas' Church, Garrison Forest
Owing Mills
MARYLAND

1 Preheat the oven to 350°. Grease and flour a 10-inch fluted tube pan; set aside.

2 To make the cake: In a medium bowl, stir together the 1 cup granulated sugar, the cocoa and the ½ cup sour milk; beat with a wire whisk until smooth; set aside.

3 In a large mixing bowl, combine the 1 cup granulated sugar and the ½ cup softened butter or margarine. Beat with an electric mixer on medium speed until the mixture is light and fluffy. Beat in the eggs.

4 In a small bowl, stir together the flour, baking soda and ½ teaspoon *salt.* In 3 parts, add the flour mixture and the 1 cup sour milk alternately to the sugar-butter mixture, beating the batter well after each addition. Add the vanilla. Beat in the cocoa mixture until all of the ingredients are well blended.

5 Pour the batter into the prepared tube pan. Bake the cake in the 350° oven for 55 minutes to 1 hour or until the top springs back when lightly touched. Let the cake cool in the pan for 15 minutes; remove from the pan. Cool the cake completely on a wire rack.

6 To make the Chocolate Glaze: In a small saucepan over low heat, melt the semisweet chocolate and the 2 tablespoons butter or margarine, stirring constantly. Remove from heat; stir in the powdered sugar and 1 tablespoon *hot water.* If necessary, stir in additional *water,* ½ teaspoon at a time, to make a drizzling consistency.

7 Spoon the Chocolate Glaze over the cooled cake.

TIPS FROM OUR KITCHEN

To make the ½ cup sour milk, pour 1½ teaspoons *vinegar* or *lemon juice* into a 1-cup measure and add enough milk to measure ½ cup. For 1 cup sour milk, use 1 tablespoon *vinegar* or *lemon juice* and add enough milk to measure 1 cup.

Chopping the chocolate that is used in the glaze helps it to melt more quickly and evenly. To chop the chocolate, use a sharp knife to cut it into small pieces.

Nutrition Analysis (*Per Serving*): Calories: 305 / Cholesterol: 63 mg / Carbohydrates: 43 g / Protein: 5 g / Sodium: 311 mg / Fat: 13 g (Saturated Fat: 8 g) / Potassium: 99 mg.

CHOCOLATE DEVIL'S FOOD CAKE

MOM'S CHOCOLATE ROLL

MOM'S CHOCOLATE ROLL

Makes 10 Servings
Cake:
- 1 cup sifted powdered sugar
- ¼ cup sifted cake flour
- ¼ cup unsweetened cocoa powder
- 5 eggs, separated
- 1 teaspoon vanilla
- 2 tablespoons granulated sugar

Sifted powdered sugar

Cream Chantilly:
- ½ cup sifted powdered sugar
- 1 teaspoon vanilla
- 2 tablespoons Amaretto (optional)
- 1 cup whipping cream, whipped

◆ ◆ ◆

Denny Buckalew told us, "My mom makes it; I just eat it." He was talking about Mom's Chocolate Roll, a treat he has enjoyed for about 25 years. Dale Crane, Denny's mom, has been making her acclaimed cake for Christmas and birthdays ever since Denny can remember. "She makes about 15 to 20 each time and gives some as gifts and keeps some for the family." Thanks, Mom!

Denny Buckalew
History Cookbook
Montgomery County Fair
Association
Conroe
TEXAS

1 Preheat the oven to 400°. Grease a 15x10x1-inch baking pan, line it with waxed paper and grease again. Set aside. To make the cake: Sift together the 1 cup powdered sugar, the flour and cocoa powder; set aside.

2 In a large mixing bowl, beat the egg yolks and vanilla about 5 minutes or until thick and pale yellow.

3 Gradually add the flour mixture to the yolk mixture, beating until combined.

4 In another bowl, using clean beaters, beat the egg whites until soft peaks form (tips curl). Gradually add the 2 tablespoons granulated sugar, beating until stiff peaks form (tips stand straight).

5 Stir about *one-fourth* of the stiffly beaten egg whites into the yolk mixture to lighten. Fold in the remaining egg whites.

6 Spread the batter evenly in the prepared pan. Bake about 10 minutes or until the cake springs back when pressed lightly. Remove from the oven and loosen the edges of the cake with a spatula.

7 Turn the cake onto a cloth that has been generously sprinkled with additional powdered sugar. Remove the waxed paper and roll the cake and towel together from a short side as for a jelly roll. Cool on a wire rack.

8 To prepare the Cream Chantilly: Fold the ½ cup powdered sugar, the vanilla and, if using, the Amaretto into the whipped cream.

9 Reserve *½ cup* of the Cream Chantilly for a garnish. Unroll the cake and spread with the remaining Cream Chantilly to within ½ inch of the short sides. Re-roll the cake without the towel. Store the roll, seam side down, in the refrigerator. To serve, sprinkle with additional powdered sugar and garnish with the remaining Cream Chantilly.

 TIPS FROM OUR KITCHEN

Once assembled, this cake should be served within 2 hours to prevent the cream from dissolving.

Nutrition Analysis (*Per Serving*): Calories: 242 / Cholesterol: 139 mg / Carbohydrates: 28 g / Protein: 5 g / Sodium: 41 mg / Fat: 12 g (Saturated Fat: 6 g) / Potassium: 63 mg.

Makes 16 Servings
Cake:
  1 cup margarine *or* butter
  2 cups granulated sugar
  ½ cup unsweetened cocoa
      powder
Pinch salt
  4 eggs, beaten
  1 teaspoon vanilla
  1½ cups all-purpose flour
  2 cups chopped pecans
Frosting:
  ½ cup margarine *or* butter,
      melted
  ⅓ cup unsweetened cocoa
      powder
  1 1-pound box powdered sugar
      (4 to 4½ cups)
  ½ cup milk
  1 6¼-ounce package miniature
      marshmallows (4 cups)

◆   ◆   ◆

Although Mississippi Mud isn't quite as southern as pecan pie, it is definitely favored in the south. Arlene Goldstein said that she first tasted this rich chocolate and marshmallow cake at a friend's house, where "everyone went crazy over it."

Arlene Goldstein
<u>Cook & Tell</u>
Sisterhood of Temple Beth-El
Birmingham
ALABAMA

1 Preheat the oven to 350°. Grease and flour a 13x9x2-inch baking pan.

2 To make the cake: In a large saucepan, melt the 2 sticks margarine or butter. Remove from heat. In a small bowl, stir together the sugar, the ½ cup cocoa powder and the salt. Add the sugar mixture to the melted margarine or butter. Stir in the beaten eggs and vanilla. Add the flour and pecans; stir until combined.

3 Spread the batter into the prepared 13x9x2-inch pan. Bake in the 350° oven for 35 minutes.

4 Meanwhile, to prepare the frosting: In a medium saucepan, melt the ½ cup margarine or butter. Stir in the cocoa powder. Stir in *2 cups* of the powdered sugar. Add the milk and stir until smooth. Stir in enough of the remaining powdered sugar to reach a spreading consistency.

5 Spread the marshmallows over the hot cake. Let the cake stand for 10 to 15 minutes. Then, spread the frosting on top of the marshmallows. When the cake is cool, cut it into squares to serve.

 TIPS FROM OUR KITCHEN

For a thinner, bar-type dessert, bake in a greased and floured 15x10x1-inch baking pan for 20 minutes. Continue as directed.

You'll need one pound of pecans if you're shelling them yourself. Store pecans in an airtight container in the refrigerator up to 1 year and in the freezer for at least 2 years.

Nutrition Analysis (*Per Serving*): Calories: 559 / Cholesterol: 54 mg / Carbohydrates: 75 g / Protein: 6 g / Sodium: 234 mg / Fat: 28 g (Saturated Fat: 4 g) / Potassium: 102 mg.

MISSISSIPPI MUD

BLITZ TORTE

BLITZ TORTE

Makes 12 Servings
Cake:
½ cup sugar
¼ cup shortening
4 egg yolks
1 cup all-purpose flour
2 teaspoons baking powder
¼ teaspoon salt
¼ cup milk
1 teaspoon vanilla
Meringue:
4 egg whites
1 teaspoon vanilla
¾ cup sugar
½ cup finely chopped pecans
Filling:
2 cups whipped cream
¼ cup sugar
1 cup sliced strawberries *or*
whole raspberries

♦ ♦ ♦

Many years ago, Pat Flanagan's great-grandmother began making "Blitz Kuchen" for Easter Sunday dessert and a special tradition was born. The torte continues to be a "very important family dessert to this day." Pat renamed the cake "Blitz Torte," and we are delighted to bring this recipe—so full of warm and wonderful family memories—to you.

Pat Kinney Flanagan
<u>*Cook's Collage*</u>
The Junior League of Tulsa
Tulsa
OKLAHOMA

1 Preheat oven to 350°. Grease and flour two 8-inch round pans.

2 To make the cake: In a medium mixing bowl, beat the sugar and shortening with an electric mixer until they are well combined. Beat in the egg yolks, one at a time. In a small bowl, stir together the flour, baking powder and salt.

3 Beat the flour mixture, *one third* at a time, into the egg yolk mixture, alternating with the milk and vanilla. (The batter will be very thick.)

4 Scrape the batter into the prepared pans, spreading the batter evenly; set the pans aside.

5 To make the meringue: In a large mixing bowl, using an electric mixer with clean beaters, beat the egg whites and vanilla until soft peaks form. Gradually beat in the sugar until it is dissolved and the mixture forms stiff peaks.

6 Carefully spread the meringue on top of the batter in the pans; sprinkle with the pecans. Bake the layers in the 350° oven for 20 minutes. Cool for 10 minutes in the pans, then remove the

layers to wire racks to cool completely. (The meringue will rise quite high during baking, then will fall as the layers cool.)

7 To make the filling: Stir together the whipped cream and the sugar.

8 Place one cake layer on a cake plate. Spread with *half* the whipped cream mixture; top with *half* the berries. Top with the second cake layer and spread with *half* the remaining whipped cream. Sprinkle with remaining berries and spread remaining whipped cream on top. Store the cake in the refrigerator until serving time.

 TIPS FROM OUR KITCHEN

Because this torte has a meringue on top of each cake layer, we found that it doesn't work to use the standard toothpick test to check for doneness. Be sure to follow the baking time exactly; the meringue should be golden brown, but not overly brown.

If desired, garnish with fresh strawberries, mint leaves and lemon leaves.

Nutrition Analysis (*Per Serving*): Calories: 295 / Cholesterol: 99 mg / Carbohydrates: 34 g / Protein: 4 g / Sodium: 124 mg / Fat: 17 g (Saturated Fat: 6 g) / Potassium: 93 mg.

Hazelnut Torte

Makes 12 Servings
Cake:
  6   egg yolks
  1   cup sugar
  ¼   cup all-purpose flour
  1   teaspoon baking powder
  ¼   teaspoon salt
  2   tablespoons rum *or* rum flavoring
  3   cups ground hazelnuts (filberts)
  6   egg whites
  ½   cup sugar
Filling:
  1   cup whipping cream, whipped
  2   tablespoons powdered sugar
  1   teaspoon rum *or* rum flavoring
Frosting:
  1   cup milk chocolate pieces, melted
  ½   cup dairy sour cream

◆ ◆ ◆

Over the years, Camp McCormick has been the source of fond memories for countless Girl Scouts. The Rock River Valley Council is committed to renovating, upgrading and expanding the camp facilities. Proceeds from the sale of <u>River Valley Recipes</u> sales are used for this purpose.

<u>River Valley Recipes</u>
Rock River Valley Council of
Girl Scouts, Inc.
Rockford
ILLINOIS

1 Preheat the oven to 350°. Lightly grease three 8x1½-inch round cake pans. Line the bottoms of the pans with waxed paper. Grease the papers and set the prepared pans aside.

2 To make the cake: In a large mixing bowl, beat the egg yolks with an electric mixer on high speed about 4 minutes or until they are thick and light-colored. Gradually beat in the 1 cup sugar.

3 In a small bowl, stir together the flour, baking powder and salt. Stir the flour mixture into the egg mixture. Add the 2 tablespoons rum or rum flavoring. Fold in the hazelnuts; set aside.

4 In a clean, medium mixing bowl, using clean beaters, beat the egg whites until soft peaks form (tips curl). Gradually add the ½ cup sugar and beat until stiff peaks form (tips stand straight).

5 Stir about *one third* (one cup) of the egg whites into the yolk mixture to lighten it. Gently fold in the remaining egg whites.

6 Spoon the batter into the prepared pans, spreading evenly. Bake in the 350° oven for 25 to 30 minutes or until a wooden toothpick inserted near the centers comes out clean.

7 Use a sharp, narrow-bladed knife to loosen the layers from the sides of the pans. Remove the layers from the pans and carefully pull off the waxed paper. Cool the layers completely on wire racks.

8 To make the filling: Stir together the whipped cream, powdered sugar and the 1 teaspoon rum or rum flavoring. Place one cake layer on a serving plate. Spread it with *half* of the whipped cream mixture, then top with another layer. Spread with the remaining whipped cream mixture and top with the last cake layer.

9 To make the frosting: Stir together the melted chocolate and sour cream. Frost the top of the cake with the chocolate mixture allowing it to drizzle down the side of the cake.

Nutrition Analysis (*Per Serving*): Calories: 493 / Cholesterol: 140 mg / Carbohydrates: 42 g / Protein: 9 g / Sodium: 129 mg / Fat: 34 g (Saturated Fat: 8 g) / Potassium: 238 mg.

HAZELNUT TORTE

FRESH ORANGE CAKE—PROPOSAL CAKE

FRESH ORANGE CAKE—PROPOSAL CAKE

Makes 12 Servings
Cake:
2¼	cups sifted cake flour
1½	cups sugar
2	teaspoons baking powder
½	teaspoon salt
¼	teaspoon baking soda
½	cup shortening

Grated rind of 1 orange (1 table-spoon or more)
¾	cup milk *or* water
¼	cup orange juice
2	eggs

Filling and Frosting:
1	cup milk
5	tablespoons sifted cake flour
½	cup shortening
½	cup butter *or* margarine, softened
1	cup granulated sugar
¼	teaspoon salt
1	teaspoon vanilla
1	cup finely chopped walnuts
½ to 1	cup sifted powdered sugar

✦　✦　✦

Elaine Holcomb's mom began making this cake in the late 1940s, and now Elaine makes it for special family get-togethers. The nickname, "Proposal Cake," comes from a spontaneous marriage proposal that was bestowed upon Elaine by a co-worker after he tasted the cake.

Elaine D. Holcomb
Taste Tested Recipes from South
United Methodist Church
Manchester
CONNECTICUT

1 Preheat the oven to 350°. Grease and flour two 8-inch round baking pans. Set aside.

2 To make the cake: Sift the dry ingredients into a large mixing bowl. Add the shortening and the grated orange rind.

3 Add the milk or water and the orange juice to the dry ingredients and beat with an electric mixer on low speed until moistened. Beat for 2 minutes at medium speed. Add the eggs; beat for an additional 2 minutes.

4 Pour the batter into the prepared cake pans. Bake in the 350° oven about 25 minutes or until the cake tests done with a wooden toothpick.

5 Cool 10 minutes, then carefully remove the cake from the pans (may stick on bottom). Cool the layers on racks.

6 To make the filling and frosting: Blend the milk and cake flour in a saucepan. Cook over medium-low heat to a very thick paste, stirring constantly. Cool to lukewarm about 40 minutes.

7 Meanwhile, in small mixing bowl, cream the shortening and butter or margarine with the 1 cup granulated sugar and salt.

8 Add the lukewarm paste to the shortening mixture and beat with electric mixer on high speed until fluffy.

9 Stir in vanilla. Remove *3/4 cup* of the mixture. (For its use, see tips below.) Fold the chopped nuts into the remaining mixture. Spread *1½ cups* of the mixture between the cake layers.

10 Add the powdered sugar to the remaining mixture and beat vigorously with a spoon to desired consistency. Frost top and sides of cake.

 TIPS FROM OUR KITCHEN

If the filling and frosting is a little soft, add some sifted powdered sugar until it is just the right spreading consistency.

If stray crumbs always seem to mess up the frosting on your cakes, try this tip. First, brush off as many crumbs as you can by hand. Then, spread the sides of the cake with a thin smooth coat of frosting. (This is where the reserved frosting is used.) This layer will help seal in any stray crumbs. Finally, spread a thicker layer of frosting over the thin layer, swirling the frosting decoratively.

Nutrition Analysis (*Per Serving*): Calories: 567 / Cholesterol: 59 mg / Carbohydrates: 67 g / Protein: 6 g / Sodium: 307 mg / Fat: 33 g (Saturated Fat: 10 g) / Potassium: 153 mg.

CHEESECAKE SQUARES

❖   ❖   ❖

Although Celeste Johnston cannot remember where she found this recipe, she has made Cheesecake Squares for over fifteen years. Celeste also said that Cheesecake Squares travel well, and that her best friend always asks Celeste to bring these yummy treats to picnics and football games.

Celeste Johnston
<u>*Cook and Love It More*</u>
Lovett Parent Association
The Lovett School
Atlanta
GEORGIA

1 Preheat the oven to 350°.

2 In a medium mixing bowl using an electric mixer, cream together the butter or margarine and brown sugar. Add the flour and walnuts or pecans; beat until the mixture is crumbly.

3 Set aside *1 cup* of the crumb mixture for the topping. Press the remaining crumb mixture into the bottom of a 9-inch square baking pan. Bake the crust in the 350° oven for 12 minutes.

4 Meanwhile, in a large mixing bowl using the electric mixer, beat together the ¼ cup granulated sugar and the 8-ounce and 3-ounce packages softened cream cheese until the mixture is smooth. Add the egg, milk, lemon juice and vanilla; beat just until the ingredients are combined.

5 Spread the cream cheese mixture evenly over the hot crust. Sprinkle the reserved crumb mixture over the top. Bake in the 350° oven about 25 minutes or until the cheesecake is set. Remove the cheesecake from the oven; *do not* turn off the oven.

6 Meanwhile, in a small bowl, stir together the sour cream and the ¼ cup granulated sugar until well mixed. Spread the sour cream mixture over the top of the hot cheesecake. Bake for 5 minutes more. Place the baking pan on a wire rack; cool completely.

7 When the cheesecake is completely cool, cut it into 3-inch squares. Store the cheesecake squares in the refrigerator until ready to serve.

 TIPS FROM OUR KITCHEN

Use a wooden chopping bowl and chopper to chop the walnuts or pecans.

To serve the cheesecake as bar cookies, prepare and bake as directed above, but do not add the sour cream layer. Then, when the cheesecake is cool, sprinkle the top with powdered sugar and cut into 16 bars.

Garnish the cheesecake squares with fan-sliced strawberries, drained mandarin orange sections or chocolate curls.

Nutrition Analysis (*Per Square*): Calories: 406 / Cholesterol: 92 mg / Carbohydrates: 32 g / Protein: 7 g / Sodium: 198 mg / Fat: 29 g (Saturated Fat: 16 g) / Potassium: 168 mg.

CHEESECAKE SQUARES

WHITE LAYER CAKE WITH SOUR CREAM FILLING

WHITE LAYER CAKE WITH SOUR CREAM FILLING

Makes 12 Servings

Cake:

2½	cups sifted cake flour
1½	cups granulated sugar
3	teaspoons baking powder
½	teaspoon salt
½	cup shortening
1	teaspoon vanilla
4	egg whites

Cake Filling:

4	egg yolks, beaten
1	cup packed brown sugar
1	8-ounce carton dairy sour cream
2	tablespoons all-purpose flour
1	cup chopped nuts
1	teaspoon vanilla

Fluffy White Frosting:

1	cup granulated sugar
¼	teaspoon cream of tartar
2	egg whites
1	teaspoon vanilla

❖ ❖ ❖

Holly Melius has had this recipe for 35 to 40 years, and she says that it's a very simple "throw-together recipe that always turns out." Holly told us that she makes this cake for birthdays and other special occasions.

Holly Melius
South Dakota Centennial Cookbook
The South Dakota Capitol Club
Sioux Falls
SOUTH DAKOTA

1 Preheat the oven to 350°. Grease and flour two 9x1½-inch round pans; set aside.

2 To make the cake: In a large mixing bowl, combine the cake flour, the 1½ cups granulated sugar, the baking powder and the ½ teaspoon salt. Using a pastry blender or 2 knives, cut in the shortening until the pieces are the size of small peas. Add 1 cup *water* and the 1 teaspoon vanilla to the sugar mixture. Beat with an electric mixer on medium speed for 5 minutes; wash beaters.

3 In a medium mixing bowl using clean beaters, beat the 4 egg whites with the electric mixer until stiff peaks form (tips stand straight). Gently fold the stiffly beaten egg whites into the cake batter.

4 Pour the batter, divided equally, into the prepared pans. Bake in the 350° oven for 25 to 30 minutes or until a wooden toothpick inserted near the center of *each* cake comes out clean. Let the cake layers cool in the pans for 10 minutes; remove from pans. Completely cool the cakes on wire racks.

5 Meanwhile, to prepare the cake filling: In a large bowl, stir together the beaten egg yolks, brown sugar, sour cream, all-purpose flour and a pinch salt. Transfer to a medium saucepan.

6 Cook and stir the filling over medium heat until thickened and bubbly. Cook and stir for 2 minutes more. Add the nuts and the 1 teaspoon vanilla; stir well.

7 Place 1 cake on a serving platter; slip strips of waxed paper underneath. Spread the filling on top of the cake; place the remaining cake layer on top. Set aside the assembled cake.

8 To make the Fluffy White Frosting: In a medium saucepan, stir together the 1 cup granulated sugar, ⅓ cup *water* and the cream of tartar. Cook and stir until the sugar dissolves and the mixture is bubbly.

9 In a small mixing bowl, combine the 2 egg whites and the 1 teaspoon vanilla. Very slowly add the sugar mixture to the egg white mixture, beating constantly with an electric mixer on high speed about 7 minutes or until stiff peaks form (tips stand straight).

10 Frost the top and the sides of the layered cake with the Fluffy White Frosting.

Nutrition Analysis (*Per Serving*): Calories: 524 / Cholesterol: 80 mg / Carbohydrates: 78 g / Protein: 7 g / Sodium: 238 mg / Fat: 21 g (Saturated Fat: 6 g) / Potassium: 187 mg.

CHOCOLATE CHEESECAKE

Makes 10 to 12 Servings
Crust:
   1   cup graham cracker crumbs
   5   tablespoons butter *or*
       margarine, melted
   2   tablespoons sugar
Filling:
   3   eggs
   1   cup sugar
   3   8-ounce packages cream
       cheese, softened
   1   12-ounce package semi-
       sweet chocolate pieces
       (2 cups)
   1   cup dairy sour cream
  ¾   cup butter *or* margarine,
       melted
   1   teaspoon vanilla
   1   cup chopped pecans

◆   ◆   ◆

In 1989, Birmingham was named "The Most Livable City in America" by the U.S. Council of Mayors. After tasting this chocolate cheesecake, courtesy of Pearl Lewis, we can understand why! Birmingham's commitment to a progressive business environment, a vibrant cultural life and a rich heritage of Southern tradition make it a magical city indeed.

Pearl Lewis
What's Cooking In Birmingham
Temple Beth El Career Women
Birmingham
ALABAMA

1 To make the crust: combine the graham cracker crumbs with the 5 tablespoons melted butter or margarine and the 2 tablespoons sugar.

2 Press the crumb mixture over the bottom of a 9-inch springform pan. Place the pan in the refrigerator to chill.

3 Preheat oven to 325°.

4 In a large bowl, beat the eggs with the 1 cup sugar. Beat in the cream cheese until the mixture is smooth.

5 Melt the chocolate pieces in the top of a double boiler over warm water. Stir in the sour cream, the ¾ cup melted butter or margarine and the vanilla. Beat the chocolate mixture into the cream cheese mixture. Stir in the pecans.

6 Carefully pour the filling into the crust-lined pan. Then spread the filling with a rubber spatula to distribute the mixture evenly. Place the springform pan in a shallow baking pan to protect your oven in case any butter leaks out of the springform pan during baking. Place both pans in the oven.

7 Bake the cheesecake in the 325° oven about 1 hour or until the center is nearly set (a 1-inch area in the center will jiggle slightly when the cheesecake is done).

8 Cool the cheesecake on a wire rack for 10 minutes. Then use a thin metal spatula to loosen the sides of the cake from the pan as shown; this helps to keep the cheesecake edges from cracking. Cool the cheesecake on the rack for 3 hours before removing the sides of the pan. The cheesecake may fall in the center or the top may crack; this is normal. Remove the sides of the pan and chill the cheesecake thoroughly.

 TIPS FROM OUR KITCHEN

For perfect slices every time, we suggest using a very thin, sharp knife. Dip the knife into a glass of warm water before you make each cut and wipe the knife clean between cuts.

Nutrition Analysis *(Per Serving):* Calories: 833 / Cholesterol: 202 mg / Carbohydrates: 58 g / Protein: 11 g / Sodium: 503 mg / Fat: 65 g (Saturated Fat: 31 g) / Potassium: 395 mg.

CHOCOLATE CHEESECAKE

PUMPKIN WALNUT CHEESECAKE

PUMPKIN WALNUT CHEESECAKE

Makes 12 Servings

Crust:

1½	cups crushed vanilla wafers (36 to 40 wafers)
¼	cup granulated sugar
6	tablespoons butter *or* margarine, melted

Filling:

3	8-ounce packages cream cheese, softened
½	cup granulated sugar
½	cup packed brown sugar
1	16-ounce can pumpkin
1	teaspoon ground cinnamon
½	teaspoon ground nutmeg
¼	teaspoon ground cloves
5	eggs
¼	cup whipping cream

Topping:

3	tablespoons butter *or* margarine
1	cup packed brown sugar
1	cup chopped walnuts

◆   ◆   ◆

Shelby Fuqua Mark has enjoyed this recipe for Pumpkin Walnut Cheesecake for approximately twelve years. The recipe came from her grandmother, whom Shelby describes as a "real southern cook."

Shelby Fuqua Mark
Dallas SPCA Cookbook
Dallas SPCA
Dallas
TEXAS

1 Preheat the oven to 350°.

2 To prepare the crust: Combine the crushed vanilla wafers, the ¼ cup granulated sugar and the 6 tablespoons melted butter or margarine. Press the mixture firmly into the bottom and 2 inches up the sides of a 9- or 10-inch springform pan. Place the springform pan into a shallow baking pan; set aside.

3 To make the filling: In a large mixing bowl, beat the cream cheese with an electric mixer until creamy. Add the ½ cup granulated sugar and the ½ cup brown sugar. Beat the mixture until light and fluffy. Beat in the pumpkin, cinnamon, nutmeg and cloves. Add the eggs all at once and beat on low speed just until combined. Stir in the whipping cream.

4 Gently pour the cream cheese mixture on top of the crust. Bake in the 350° oven for 1 hour.

5 Meanwhile, to prepare the topping: In small mixing bowl, using a pastry blender, cut the 3 tablespoons butter or margarine into the 1 cup brown sugar. Stir in the walnuts.

6 Carefully sprinkle the mixture evenly over the hot cheesecake. Bake 25 minutes more. Cool on a wire rack for 15 minutes.

7 Using a thin metal spatula, loosen the crust from sides of the pan. Cool for 30 minutes more, then remove the sides of the pan. Cool completely. Cover and refrigerate for at least 4 hours before serving.

 TIPS FROM OUR KITCHEN

Be sure to use large eggs in this recipe. After adding the eggs, beat the mixture just until combined. Beating too vigorously will incorporate too much air, causing the cheesecake to puff and then fall, creating a crack.

Placing the springform pan in a shallow baking pan can eliminate some clean up. If the springform pan accidentally leaks, the baking pan will catch the spills.

Nutrition Analysis (*Per Serving*): Calories: 607 / Cholesterol: 189 mg / Carbohydrates: 55 g / Protein: 10 g / Sodium: 326 mg / Fat: 41 g (Saturated Fat: 21 g) / Potassium: 334 mg.

CHOCOLATE CHIP POUND CAKE

Makes 16 Servings
Cake:
- 1 cup butter *or* margarine
- 1 tablespoon shortening
- 2 cups sugar
- 6 eggs, separated
- 3 cups all-purpose flour
- ½ teaspoon salt
- ¼ teaspoon baking soda
- 1 8-ounce container dairy sour cream
- 1 teaspoon vanilla
- 1 12-ounce package semisweet chocolate pieces
- 1 4-ounce package sweet baking chocolate, grated

Glaze:
- 1 cup sifted powdered sugar
- 1 tablespoon milk

◆   ◆   ◆

After Donnie Huckaby's mother-in-law, Oleta, tried Donnie's Chocolate Chip Pound Cake, she began serving it at all the family functions. Donnie tells us that it pleased her that Oleta, who was such a good cook herself, loved the recipe. Although it wasn't originally a family recipe, "it certainly has become one."

Donnie Huckaby
Central Texas Style
Junior Service League
of Killeen, Inc.
Killeen
TEXAS

1 Preheat the oven to 325°. Grease and flour a 10-inch tube pan. Set aside.

2 To make the cake: In a large mixing bowl, cream the butter or margarine and shortening with an electric mixer. Gradually add *1½ cups* of the sugar and beat until the mixture is light and fluffy. Add the egg yolks. Beat on medium-high speed for 5 minutes.

3 In another mixing bowl, stir together the flour, salt and baking soda.

4 Add the flour mixture and sour cream to the butter mixture, alternately, beginning and ending with the flour mixture. Mix just until blended after each addition.

5 Stir in the vanilla, *1⅓ cups* of the chocolate pieces and all of the grated chocolate.

6 Using clean beaters and a clean medium mixing bowl, beat the egg whites until foamy. Gradually add the remaining *½ cup* sugar to the egg whites, beating until stiff peaks form (tips stand straight).

7 Stir *one third* of the beaten egg white mixture into the batter to lighten it. Then, carefully fold in the remaining egg white mixture.

8 Spoon the batter into the prepared pan. Bake in the 325° oven for 1 hour and 20 minutes to 1 hour and 30 minutes or until a toothpick inserted near the center comes out clean. Cool in the pan for 10 minutes, then invert onto a serving plate.

9 To make the glaze: Combine the powdered sugar and milk. Add more milk if a thinner consistency is desired. Spoon the glaze over the warm cake. Sprinkle the remaining chocolate pieces over the glaze. Cool before serving.

 TIPS FROM OUR KITCHEN

Folding—not stirring—is the way to keep beaten egg whites airy and fluffy.

There's a lot of batter for this cake, so be sure to use a large bowl in order to have enough room to fold in all the egg whites.

Nutrition Analysis *(Per Serving)*: Calories: 496 / Cholesterol: 117 mg / Carbohydrates: 66 g / Protein: 6 g / Sodium: 230 mg / Fat: 26 g (Saturated Fat: 10 g) / Potassium: 158 mg.

CHOCOLATE CHIP POUND CAKE

SWEET POTATO POUND CAKE

SWEET POTATO POUND CAKE

Makes 16 Servings
Cake:
- 1 cup butter *or* margarine, softened
- 2 cups sugar
- 2 cups cooked, mashed and cooled sweet potatoes (2 medium)
- 1 teaspoon vanilla
- 4 eggs
- 3 cups all-purpose flour
- 2 teaspoons baking powder
- 1 teaspoon ground cinnamon
- ½ teaspoon baking soda
- ½ teaspoon ground nutmeg
- ¼ teaspoon salt

Glaze:
- 1 cup sifted powdered sugar
- 3 to 5 teaspoons orange juice
- Shredded orange peel (optional)

◆   ◆   ◆

During the colonial days, cakes were difficult and costly to make, and even the gentry reserved them for holidays and special occasions. Pound Cake, a timeless favorite in the South, was so named because it was made with one pound of each ingredient. Luckily for us, it's no longer so difficult or expensive to make a scrumptious cake!

Virginia Hospitality
Junior League of Hampton Roads, Inc.
Hampton
VIRGINIA

1 Preheat the oven to 350°. Grease and flour a 10-inch tube pan. Set aside.

2 To make the cake: In a large mixing bowl, beat together the butter or margarine and sugar with an electric mixer until light and fluffy. Add the sweet potatoes and vanilla and beat until well combined.

3 Add the eggs, one at a time, beating for 1 minute after each addition. (The batter will look curdled.)

4 In a large mixing bowl, stir together the flour, baking powder, cinnamon, baking soda, nutmeg and salt. Slowly add the flour mixture to the potato mixture. Beat on low speed until just combined.

5 Pour the batter into the prepared pan. Bake in the 350° oven about 1 hour and 20 minutes or until a wooden toothpick inserted near the center of the cake comes out clean.

6 Cool the cake in the pan on a wire rack for 20 minutes, then invert onto a serving plate.

7 To make the glaze: In a small bowl, stir together the sifted powdered sugar and 1 tablespoon of the orange juice. Add enough additional orange juice (1 to 2 teaspoons) to give the glaze a drizzling consistency.

8 Spoon the glaze over the warm cake. If desired, sprinkle with orange peel. Cool completely.

 TIPS FROM OUR KITCHEN

This cake can be made in loaf pans, if you prefer. Prepare batter as directed above, *except* grease and flour four 7½x 3½x2-inch loaf pans or six 4½x2½x1½-inch loaf pans. Pour the batter into the pans. Bake in the 350° oven for 40 to 50 minutes or until a wooden toothpick inserted near the center comes out clean. Cool the cakes in the pans on wire racks for 10 minutes. Invert and glaze as directed above.

To cook sweet potatoes: Wash, peel and cut off woody portions, then cut the potatoes into quarters. Cook, covered, in enough boiling water to cover, about 25 minutes or until tender. Drain and mash until smooth using a potato masher, fork, food mill, food ricer or electric mixer.

Nutrition Analysis (*Per Serving*): Calories: 348 / Cholesterol: 84 mg / Carbohydrates: 55 g / Protein: 5 g / Sodium: 258 mg / Fat: 13 g (Saturated Fat: 8 g) / Potassium: 112.

CARROT WALNUT CAKE

Makes 12 to 16 Servings

- 3 cups all-purpose flour
- 2 teaspoons baking powder
- 1 teaspoon baking soda
- 1 teaspoon ground cinnamon
- ½ teaspoon salt
- 1 cup butter *or* margarine, softened
- 1 cup packed light brown sugar
- 1 cup granulated sugar
- 4 eggs
- 1 tablespoon grated orange peel
- 2 tablespoons orange juice
- 2 teaspoons grated lemon peel
- 2 tablespoons lemon juice
- 3 cups finely shredded carrots (1 pound)
- 1 cup coarsely chopped walnuts
- 1 cup raisins

Cream Cheese Frosting:
- 1 8-ounce package cream cheese, softened
- 1½ cups sifted powdered sugar
- 1 teaspoon grated lemon peel
- 1 tablespoon lemon juice
- ½ cup coarsely chopped walnuts (optional)
- Whole walnuts (optional)

♦   ♦   ♦

Clara Rutledge
Katz Employee
Sunshine Cookbook
Katz Employee Sunshine Club
Honesdale
PENNSYLVANIA

1 Preheat the oven to 350°. Lightly grease and flour a 10-inch tube pan; set aside.

2 In a medium mixing bowl, stir together the flour, baking powder, baking soda, cinnamon and salt; set aside.

3 In a large mixing bowl, combine the butter or margarine, brown sugar and granulated sugar. Beat with an electric mixer on medium to high speed about 4 minutes or until light and fluffy, scraping the bowl occasionally. Add the eggs, one at a time, beating well (about 1 minute) after each addition.

4 Combine the orange peel, orange juice, the 2 teaspoons lemon peel and the 2 tablespoons lemon juice. Add the juice and the flour mixtures alternately to the butter-sugar mixture, beginning and ending with the flour mixture. After each addition, beat at low speed just until smooth.

5 Using a wooden spoon, stir in the carrots, walnuts and raisins. Mix well.

6 Pour the batter into the prepared pan, spreading evenly. Bake in the 350° oven for 60 to 65 minutes or until a wooden toothpick inserted near the center comes out clean.

7 Cool the cake in the pan on a wire rack for 20 minutes. Then, loosen the edge of the cake and remove it from the pan. Cool completely on the wire rack.

8 Meanwhile, to make the Cream Cheese Frosting: In a medium mixing bowl, combine the softened cream cheese, powdered sugar, the 1 teaspoon lemon peel and the 1 tablespoon lemon juice. Beat with an electric mixer on medium speed until smooth and creamy, scraping the sides of the bowl as needed.

9 When cool, carefully transfer the cake to a serving plate. Spread with the frosting. Decorate with the chopped walnuts and the whole walnuts, if desired. Store the cake, tightly covered, in the refrigerator until serving time.

TIPS FROM OUR KITCHEN

Use a fine—not coarse—grater for the carrots so the flavor and moisture are evenly distributed throughout the cake. A food processor also works well for this purpose.

If desired, for the garnish, sift the nuts after chopping them to remove the fine particles.

Nutrition Analysis (*Per Serving*): Calories: 659 / Cholesterol: 133 mg / Carbohydrates: 86 g / Protein: 10 g / Sodium: 457 mg / Fat: 33 g (Saturated Fat: 15 g) / Potassium: 398 mg.

CARROT WALNUT CAKE

PUMPKIN CAKE

PUMPKIN CAKE

Makes 9 Servings
- ½ cup shortening
- 1¼ cups sugar
- 2 eggs
- 1¼ cups sifted cake flour
- 1 tablespoon baking powder
- ½ teaspoon salt
- ½ teaspoon ground cinnamon
- ½ teaspoon ground ginger
- ½ teaspoon ground nutmeg
- 1 cup cooked and cooled fresh pumpkin *or* 1 cup canned pumpkin
- ¾ cup milk
- ½ teaspoon baking soda
- ½ cup chopped nuts
- Raisin-Brown Sugar Icing

◆ ◆ ◆

By the age of 12 in 1904, Elva McGahuey was cooking for the large wheat and apple harvest crews in Eastern Washington. Later, her daughter Hazel stood beside her with pen in hand as Elva prepared the meals on a woodstove using no recipes. Pumpkin Cake is one of the recipes that Hazel wrote down, enabling us to share in this extraordinary taste of history today.

Hazel DeLorenzo
Fiddlin' in the Kitchen
The Chamber Music Society of Oregon
Portland
OREGON

1 Preheat oven to 350°. Grease and flour a 9x9x2-inch baking pan. Line the bottom with waxed paper. Set aside.

2 To make the cake: In a large mixing bowl, cream the shortening. Gradually add the sugar, beating until light and fluffy. Beat in the eggs.

3 In a medium bowl, sift together the cake flour, baking powder, salt, cinnamon, ginger and nutmeg.

4 Combine the pumpkin and milk. Stir in the baking soda.

5 Add the flour and pumpkin mixtures alternately to the shortening-sugar mixture, beating well after each addition. Fold in nuts. Turn the batter into the prepared baking pan.

 TIPS FROM OUR KITCHEN

Don't add the baking soda to the pumpkin-milk mixture until you're ready to combine it with the flour mixture. Otherwise, the soda will lose much of its leavening power.

6 Bake in the 350° oven for 50 minutes. Cool in the pan on a wire rack for 10 minutes. Turn the cake out onto the rack; remove the waxed paper and cool completely. Frost the top and sides with the Raisin-Brown Sugar Icing.

7 Raisin-Brown Sugar Icing: In the top of a double boiler, beat together 1 large *egg white*, 1 cup packed *light brown sugar* and 3 tablespoons *water* just until blended. Place the mixture over rapidly boiling water and beat with a rotary beater or an electric mixer for 5 to 7 minutes, or until the mixture is light and fluffy and holds stiff peaks.

8 Remove from the heat. Carefully fold in ½ cup *coarsely chopped raisins*.

Don't be surprised or worried if the icing thins a little when you add the raisins.

Nutrition Analysis (*Per Serving*): Calories: 430 / Cholesterol: 49 mg / Carbohydrates: 69 g / Protein: 5 g / Sodium: 301 mg / Fat: 17 g (Saturated Fat: 4 g) / Potassium: 244 mg.

APPLESAUCE CAKE

Makes 16 Servings

2½	cups all-purpose flour
2	cups sugar
1	teaspoon baking soda
1	teaspoon baking powder
¾	teaspoon ground cinnamon
½	teaspoon salt
½	teaspoon ground allspice
¼	teaspoon ground cloves
1½	cups applesauce
½	cup shortening
½	cup cold water
2	eggs
1	cup raisins
½	cup chopped walnuts

Cream Cheese Frosting (optional)

❖   ❖   ❖

When the creators began to develop **Terry Home Presents Food & Fun From Celebrities & Us**, *they wrote to several celebrities asking for recipe submissions. They received 33 responses and began the 1½-year-long project of creating the cookbook. Now,* **Food & Fun** *is on the market and successfully raising funds for Terry Home, Inc.*

Annette Woods
Terry Home Presents Food & Fun From Celebrities & Us
Terry Home, Inc.
Auburn
WASHINGTON

1 Preheat the oven to 350°. Grease a 13x9x2-inch baking pan; set aside.

2 In a large mixing bowl, stir together the flour, sugar, baking soda, baking powder, cinnamon, salt, allspice and cloves.

3 Add the applesauce, shortening and cold water to the flour mixture. Beat with an electric mixer on low speed until the mixture is blended. Increase the speed to medium and beat for 2 minutes, scraping the sides of the bowl. Add the eggs and beat for 2 minutes more. Stir in the raisins and walnuts.

4 Turn the batter into the prepared baking pan. Bake in the 350° oven for 45 to 50 minutes or until a wooden toothpick inserted near the center of the cake comes out clean. Set the pan on a wire rack; cool completely. If desired, frost with Cream Cheese Frosting.

 TIPS FROM OUR KITCHEN

To make Cream Cheese Frosting: In a medium mixing bowl using an electric mixer, beat together two 3-ounce packages softened *cream cheese*, ½ cup softened *butter* or *margarine* and 2 teaspoons *vanilla* until the mixture is light and fluffy. Gradually add 2 cups sifted *powdered sugar*, beating well. Beat in ½ teaspoon *ground cinnamon* and ¼ teaspoon *ground nutmeg*. Gradually add up to 2¾ cups additional sifted *powdered sugar* until the frosting is a good spreading consistency. Spread over the cooled cake. Cover the frosted cake with plastic wrap and store it in the refrigerator.

To cut this cake into wedge-shaped pieces: Cut the cake in half crosswise; cut *each half* in half crosswise again. Then, cut the cake in half lengthwise to form eight rectangles. To serve, cut each rectangle in half diagonally.

The batter for this cake will be thick. For the best volume, use room temperature applesauce and let the eggs sit at room temperature up to 30 minutes before mixing.

If you use a glass baking dish instead of a metal baking pan, reduce the oven temperature to 325°.

To bake this recipe as snack-ready cupcakes, grease 24 muffin cups or line with paper bake cups; spoon in the batter, filling each halfway. Bake in the 350° oven for 18 to 23 minutes or until a wooden toothpick inserted near the centers comes out clean.

If you wish, you might sprinkle powdered sugar over the top instead of frosting the cake.

Nutrition Analysis (*Per Serving*): Calories: 284 / Cholesterol: 27 mg / Carbohydrates: 48 g / Protein: 4 g / Sodium: 153 mg / Fat: 10 g (Saturated Fat: 2 g) / Potassium: 123 mg.

APPLESAUCE CAKE

GINGERBREAD CAKE

GINGERBREAD CAKE

◆   ◆   ◆

In 1963 Fr. John Guidera's family and a handful of friends established a Dollar-A-Month Club to support his work in India. "The purpose of the club was to bring together peoples of two worlds and, by mutually sharing, come to a deeper love and appreciation for each other." Continuing its support today, the club has grown to 850 members and this cook-book is its largest fund-raiser.

Ann Canter
The Dollar-A-Month Club
Anniversary Cookbook: A
Collection of Recipes to Celebrate
the Year
The Jesuit Jamshedpur Mission
Baltimore
MARYLAND

1 Preheat the oven to 350°. Grease and flour a 10-inch fluted tube pan; set aside.

2 In a large mixing bowl, combine the molasses, sugar, melted margarine or butter and eggs. Beat with an electric mixer on medium speed about 1 minute or until the mixture is smooth.

3 In a large bowl, stir together the flour, baking soda, ginger, cinnamon, nutmeg, cloves and ¼ teaspoon *salt*.

4 Add the flour mixture to the egg mixture alternately with 1¼ cups *boiling water*, beating on low speed just until smooth (the batter will be thin). Pour the batter into the prepared pan.

5 Bake in the 350° oven for 40 to 50 minutes or until the top of the cake springs back when lightly touched and a wooden toothpick inserted near the center of the cake comes out clean.

6 Set the pan on a wire rack; cool for 15 minutes. Invert the pan; remove the cake and cool completely on the wire rack. If desired, sprinkle with the powdered sugar by holding a sifter or sieve over the cake and spooning in the powdered sugar. Then, gently shake the sieve or squeeze the sifter over the cake until the top is lightly dusted with the powdered sugar.

 TIPS FROM OUR KITCHEN

Use a pastry brush to evenly distribute shortening over the bottom and up the sides of the cake pan. Sprinkle about 1 tablespoon of flour into the pan. Shake the pan until the greased areas are completely coated with the flour, adding additional flour if necessary. Pour out any extra flour.

Before inverting the pan onto the wire rack, use a flexible knife or metal spatula to loosen the center and sides of the cake from the tube pan. If necessary, to further loosen the cake, lightly tap the pan.

Orange Sauce is one traditional topping for gingerbread. To make Orange Sauce in the microwave: In a 2-cup measure, stir together ¼ cup *granulated sugar*, 1 tablespoon *cornstarch* and ¼ teaspoon finely shredded *orange peel*. Stir in ¾ cup *orange juice*. Micro-cook, uncovered, on 100% power (high) for 2 to 3 minutes or until the mixture is bubbly, stirring once during the cooking time. Stir in 2 teaspoons *margarine* or *butter*. Serve warm. Makes ¾ cup.

Nutrition Analysis (*Per Serving*): Calories: 473 / Cholesterol: 64 mg / Carbohydrates: 68 g / Protein: 6 g / Sodium: 531 mg / Fat: 20 g (Saturated Fat: 4 g) / Potassium: 367 mg.

HUMMINGBIRD CAKE

Makes 12 Servings
Cake:

3	cups all-purpose flour
2	cups sugar
1	teaspoon ground cinnamon
1	teaspoon baking soda
½	teaspoon salt
1	8-ounce can crushed pineapple with juice
1	cup cooking oil
3	large eggs, well beaten
2	cups chopped banana (3 bananas)
½	cup finely chopped walnuts *or* pecans
1½	teaspoons vanilla

Glaze:

1	tablespoon melted butter *or* margarine
1	cup sifted powdered sugar

❖   ❖   ❖

This delicious Victorian cake recipe has been passed down to Bobbie Shinners from her friend, Mrs. Bonnie Wells. Bobbie says that she "just fell in love with it!" She loves the taste and says that it is a favorite dish to bring to gatherings because it freezes well and serves so many. Friends and family are always asking her for the recipe.

Bobbie Shinners
What's Cooking in Philadelphia
The Philadelphia Rotary Club
Philadelphia
PENNSYLVANIA

1 Preheat oven to 325°. Generously grease a 10-inch tube or fluted tube pan.

2 To make the cake: In a large mixing bowl, stir together the flour, sugar, cinnamon, baking soda and salt.

3 Remove *2 tablespoons* of the juice from the can of pineapple. Set aside for the glaze.

4 Add the pineapple, oil, eggs, banana, nuts and vanilla to the flour mixture. Stir until just blended (do not beat).

5 Pour the batter into the prepared pan. Bake in the 325° oven about 1 hour and 10 minutes or until a wooden toothpick inserted near the center comes out clean. Cool in the pan for 15 minutes. Invert the cake onto a wire rack and remove the cake from the pan. Cool completely.

6 To make the glaze: In a small mixing bowl, combine the melted butter or margarine and the powdered sugar. Add enough of the reserved pineapple juice to make a glaze of drizzling consistency. Drizzle the glaze over the cooled cake.

 TIPS FROM OUR KITCHEN

To evenly grease a fluted tube pan, use a pastry brush to coat the pan with shortening.

For a glaze with a whole new dimension, substitute rum for the pineapple juice.

Nutrition Analysis *(Per Serving)*: Calories: 516 / Cholesterol: 56 mg / Carbohydrates: 73 g / Protein: 6 g / Sodium: 185 mg / Fat: 24 g (Saturated Fat: 4 g) / Potassium: 208 mg.

HUMMINGBIRD CAKE

PINEAPPLE UPSIDE-DOWN CAKE

PINEAPPLE UPSIDE-DOWN CAKE

Makes 10 Servings

Topping:

1	8-ounce can pineapple slices
2	tablespoons butter *or* margarine
⅓	cup packed brown sugar
8	maraschino cherries, halved
¼	cup pecan halves

Cake:

6	tablespoons butter *or* margarine
1	cup granulated sugar
2	eggs
1½	cups all-purpose flour
1	teaspoon baking powder
½	teaspoon salt
½	cup milk
½	teaspoon vanilla
¼	teaspoon lemon extract

◆ ◆ ◆

Katherine Taylor's mother-in-law gave her this wonderful recipe for Pineapple Upside-Down Cake about 35 years ago. Katherine says that this is a favorite of her husband's—the one he always requests. She said that she couldn't wait to tell him that his favorite cake is included in this series!

Katherine Taylor
Laboratory Approved Recipes
Pathology Laboratories Wake Medical Center
Raleigh
NORTH CAROLINA

1 To make the topping: Drain the pineapple slices, reserving the juice. Measure the juice and add *water* to make ½ cup. Set aside.

2 In a 10-inch skillet with an oven-safe handle and straight sides, melt the 2 tablespoons butter or margarine. Stir in the brown sugar and pineapple juice. Bring to a boil. Cook and stir about 7 minutes or until the mixture is thickened. Remove from heat. Spread the syrup evenly over the bottom of the skillet; cool.

3 Arrange the pineapple slices, maraschino cherries and pecans over the syrup mixture; set aside. Preheat the oven to 350°.

4 To make the cake: In a large mixing bowl, combine the 6 tablespoons butter or margarine and the granulated sugar. Beat with an electric mixer on medium speed until well blended, scraping sides of bowl. Beat in the eggs.

5 In a small mixing bowl, stir together the flour, baking powder and salt. Add the flour mixture and the milk alternately to the creamed mixture, beating well after each addition.

6 Stir in the vanilla and lemon extract. Carefully pour the batter over the syrup mixture in the skillet, spreading to reach the edges. Bake in the 350° oven about 30 minutes or until a wooden toothpick inserted near the center comes out clean.

7 Cool a few minutes in the skillet. Carefully invert the cake onto a serving platter.

 TIPS FROM OUR KITCHEN

If you don't have lemon extract, use more vanilla instead. Or, for a change, try pineapple extract instead of the lemon extract.

If your skillet has a wooden handle, wrap it in aluminum foil to protect it from the oven heat. Or, transfer the brown sugar-and-pineapple mixture to a 12x7½x2-inch baking pan.

Maraschino cherries are made by preserving and dying yellow sweet cherries such as Royal Ann, Rainier and Golden Bing varieties.

Nutrition Analysis (*Per Serving*): Calories: 302 / Cholesterol: 68 mg / Carbohydrates: 46 g / Protein: 4 g / Sodium: 223 mg / Fat: 12 g (Saturated Fat: 6 g) / Potassium: 126 mg.

OLD-FASHIONED STRAWBERRY SHORTCAKE

Makes 12 Servings
Shortcakes:

3	cups all-purpose flour
¼	cup sugar
3½	teaspoons baking powder
½	teaspoon salt
½	cup shortening, butter *or* margarine
1	cup milk
2	tablespoons melted butter *or* margarine
2	tablespoons softened butter *or* margarine (optional)

Topping:

2	quarts fresh strawberries, hulled, rinsed and sliced (8 cups) *or* three 10-ounce packages frozen strawberries, thawed
1	cup heavy whipping cream, whipped

❖ ❖ ❖

"In addition to the Derby, Kentucky is famous for its good cooks," says Irene Hayes, cookbook chairperson for <u>What's Cooking in Kentucky</u>. Profits from the sale of the cookbook, now in its third edition, are given to a local church to help pay for needed renovations.

Alice Hayes
<u>What's Cooking in Kentucky:</u>
<u>Treasured Old Recipes and the</u>
<u>Best of the New</u>
T.I. Hayes Publishing Company
Ft. Mitchell
KENTUCKY

1 Preheat the oven to 450°.

2 To make the shortcakes: In a large mixing bowl, stir together the flour, sugar, baking powder and salt. Using a pastry blender, cut in the shortening, butter or margarine until the mixture resembles coarse crumbs.

3 Add the milk to the flour mixture and stir just until moistened.

4 Turn the dough out onto a lightly floured surface and knead about 20 times.

5 Roll or pat the dough out to a ¼-inch thickness. With a 3-inch round cutter, cut the dough into circles. Place *half* of the circles on an ungreased baking sheet and brush them well with the 2 tablespoons melted butter or margarine. Top with the remaining dough circles.

6 Bake the shortcakes in the 450° oven for 10 to 12 minutes or until golden brown. Remove from the oven.

7 To assemble: Separate the shortcake halves and spread them with the 2 tablespoons softened butter or margarine, if desired. Place the bottom halves on serving plates. Spoon *half* of the strawberries over the bottom halves of the shortcakes. Layer on the top halves of the shortcakes. Spoon on the remaining strawberries. Serve while the shortcakes are still warm, topped with the whipped cream.

 TIPS FROM OUR KITCHEN

If you don't have a round cutter, pat the dough into a rectangle and use a sharp knife to cut 3-inch squares.

You can make the shortcakes using an alternative method. Knead the dough and roll out or pat to a ½-inch thickness. Cut and bake the biscuits as directed. Before assembling, split the biscuits in half and proceed with the assembly.

For a juicier strawberry topping, combine the strawberries and 2 to 4 tablespoons *sugar* (depending on the natural sweetness of the berries) and let stand for 10 to 15 minutes to allow the mixture to become juicy. Lightly mash about half of the berries, then stir all of the berries together.

Nutrition Analysis (*Per Serving*): Calories: 349 / Cholesterol: 39 mg / Carbohydrates: 37 g / Protein: 5 g / Sodium: 158 mg / Fat: 21 g (Saturated Fat: 9 g) / Potassium: 248 mg.

OLD-FASHIONED STRAWBERRY SHORTCAKE

CREAM PUFFS

CREAM PUFFS

Makes 8 to 10 Servings
Puffs:
  1 cup water
  ½ cup butter *or* margarine
  1 cup all-purpose flour
  4 eggs, beaten
Vanilla Cream Pudding:
  ½ cup granulated sugar
  3 tablespoons cornstarch
  ⅛ teaspoon salt
  3 cups milk
  3 egg yolks, slightly beaten
  3 tablespoons butter *or*
     margarine
  2 teaspoons vanilla
  Powdered sugar (optional)

◆ ◆ ◆

Tamara Putney received the recipe for Cream Puffs about 10 to 15 years ago at a homemakers' meeting at her church. At the meetings, members took turns giving cooking lessons or sharing crafts. During one of these lessons, the recipe for Cream Puffs was presented. Tamara said that she makes these treats mostly for her children, although they can be served easily at parties. "They're fast and easy to make."

Tamara Putney
Harrington Cooks
Harrington Homemakers
Harrington
WASHINGTON

1 Preheat the oven to 400°. Lightly grease a baking sheet; set aside.

2 To make the puffs: In a large heavy saucepan, bring the water and the ½ cup butter or margarine to a rolling boil. Stir in the flour. Reduce heat to low and stir the mixture vigorously until it forms a ball. Remove the saucepan from the heat; set aside to cool for 10 minutes.

3 Add the 4 beaten eggs all at once to the flour mixture. Continue beating until the pastry dough is smooth.

4 Using a scant *½ cup* for *each* puff, drop the dough 3 inches apart onto the prepared baking sheet.

5 Bake in the 400° oven for 35 to 40 minutes or until the puffs are firm and golden. Transfer the puffs to wire racks to cool.

6 Meanwhile, to make the Vanilla Cream Pudding: In a 2-quart saucepan, stir together the granulated sugar, cornstarch and salt. In a small bowl, stir together the milk and the 3 slightly beaten egg yolks. Gradually add the milk mixture to the sugar mixture, stirring well.

7 Cook over medium heat, stirring constantly, until the mixture is thickened and bubbly. Reduce heat and cook for 2 minutes more, stirring constantly. Remove the saucepan from the heat and stir in the 3 tablespoons butter or margarine and the vanilla. Cover the saucepan with plastic wrap or waxed paper and refrigerate; do not stir the pudding as it chills.

8 To assemble the Cream Puffs: Cut each puff in half and remove the webbing. Spoon *some* of the Vanilla Cream Pudding into the bottom half of *each* puff. Replace the tops. Sprinkle with the powdered sugar, if desired.

 TIPS FROM OUR KITCHEN

Fill the cream puffs no more than 2 hours before serving or they'll become soggy. Keep the filled puffs refrigerated until you are ready to serve them.

Baked cream puff shells should be stored in airtight containers in the refrigerator up to 24 hours or frozen up to 2 months. Then thaw them at room temperature for 5 to 10 minutes.

Nutrition Analysis (*Per Serving*): Calories: 360 / Cholesterol: 235 mg / Carbohydrates: 31 g / Protein: 9 g / Sodium: 274 mg / Fat: 23 g (Saturated Fat: 12 g) / Potassium: 198 mg.

FROZEN RAINBOW DESSERT

Makes 16 Servings

- 2 cups heavy whipping cream
- 3 tablespoons sugar
- 1 teaspoon vanilla
- 3 cups coconut macaroon crumbs (about 15 cookies)
- 1 cup chopped walnuts
- 1 pint orange sherbet, softened
- 1 pint lime sherbet, softened
- 1 pint raspberry sherbet, softened

❖ ❖ ❖

This recipe for Frozen Rainbow Dessert has been in Bev Solheim's family for so long that she can't even begin to remember its origin. Bev tells us that the dessert is a nice, light ending to any meal and that children especially love it for its colorful presentation and fruity taste. For a change with a little bit of tang, Bev occasionally substitutes pineapple or lemon sherbet for one of the sherbets listed in the recipe.

Bev Solheim
Redeemer Lutheran Church
Favorite Recipes
Thief River Falls
MINNESOTA

1 Lightly oil an 11- to 12-cup mold. Invert the mold to drain the excess oil.

2 In a large mixing bowl, beat the whipping cream, sugar and vanilla with an electric mixer until stiff peaks form (tips stand straight). Combine the macaroon crumbs with the walnuts. Fold the crumb-nut mixture into the whipped cream.

3 Spread *half* of the whipped cream mixture evenly in the bottom of the mold. Freeze until firm. Refrigerate the remaining whipped cream mixture.

4 Layer the orange, lime and raspberry sherbets on top of the whipped cream layer. As necessary, place the mold in the freezer between adding the layers to prevent the layers from running together.

5 Top with the remaining whipped cream mixture.

6 Cover and freeze at least 6 hours. To unmold, briefly dip the mold in *hot* water and invert onto a platter.

TIPS FROM OUR KITCHEN

To soften the sherbet for easier spreading, place it in a chilled bowl. Working with a wooden spoon, press the sherbet against the sides of the bowl. Work quickly so the sherbet doesn't melt.

For nice, even layers that don't run together, freeze the dessert at least 20 minutes after adding each flavor of sherbet.

Using a cake pan with a removable bottom, such as as angel-food cake pan or a springform pan, makes unmolding this dessert easier.

To make slicing this frozen dessert easy, dip your knife in hot water between cuts.

Nutrition Analysis *(Per Serving)*: Calories: 346 / Cholesterol: 46 mg / Carbohydrates: 38 g / Protein: 3 g / Sodium: 51 mg / Fat: 21 g (Saturated Fat: 8 g) / Potassium: 217 mg.

FROZEN RAINBOW DESSERT

pies &
puddings

If there is such a thing as Pie In The Sky, this selection of pastry perfections would shine as the brightest in the galaxy. The heavenly concoctions include such stellar recipes as Lemon Luscious Pie, rich and creamy Chocolate Chess Pie, and picture-perfect Peanut Butter Pie. Tried-and-true favorites are glowingly represented by Fresh Blueberry Pie and Georgia's Pecan Pie; radiant newcomers include Fudge Sundae Pie and a yummy Apple Dessert Pancake. You'll also find superb puddings, such as Jul Grot—Sweden's take on rice pudding—and tangy Lemon Cups. Serve any of these sparkling sweets and make your dinner table heavenly.

CHOCOLATE CHESS PIE

CHOCOLATE CHESS PIE

Makes 8 Servings

- 1½ cups sugar
- 3 tablespoons unsweetened cocoa powder
- 2 eggs, beaten
- 1 5-ounce can (⅔ cup) evaporated milk
- ¼ cup margarine *or* butter, melted
- 1 teaspoon vanilla
- Dash salt
- 1 9-inch unbaked pie shell

◆　◆　◆

Mary Lynne collects recipes with an emphasis on minimum effort and fantastic results. For these reasons, she brings us Chocolate Chess Pie. For variety, Mary Lynne sometimes adds peppermint chips or peanut butter chips. At Christmastime, she uses this basic recipe to make tarts wreathed in whipped cream and garnished with green sugar sprinkles and red hots.

Mary Lynne Courtney
Potluck
The Women's Center
Raleigh
NORTH CAROLINA

1 Preheat oven to 325°.

2 In a medium mixing bowl, stir together the sugar and the cocoa. Add the eggs, evaporated milk, melted margarine or butter, vanilla and salt.

3 Carefully pour the mixture into a pastry-lined tart pan or pie plate. Bake in the 325° oven about 50 minutes or until puffed over the entire surface. Cool on a wire rack.

TIPS FROM OUR KITCHEN

Prebaking the pastry will help make the crust deliciously flaky. Here's how to do it: Once you've positioned the pastry in the tart pan or pie plate, line the unpricked shell with a double thickness of heavy-duty foil. Bake it in a 450° oven for 5 minutes. Remove the foil. Bake for 5 to 7 minutes more or until the pastry is nearly done. Remove the pastry from the oven and reduce the oven temperature to 325°. Then add the filling and proceed according to this recipe.

For a lovely presentation, garnish each piece of the pie with some piped whipped cream and a little shaved milk chocolate.

For a dessert truly "made in heaven," top this brownie-like pie with a scoop of butter pecan or other nut-flavored ice cream.

Nutrition Analysis (*Per Serving*): Calories: 382 / Cholesterol: 59 mg / Carbohydrates: 53 g / Protein: 5 g / Sodium: 187 mg / Fat: 17 g (Saturated Fat: 5 g) / Potassium: 97 mg.

PARTY CHOCOLATE PIE

◆   ◆   ◆

Lois French's sister-in-law gave her the recipe for Party Chocolate Pie about forty-five years ago. The original recipe called for unspecified nuts, so Lois began experimenting. Eventually, she found that she liked slivered almonds the best. Lois tells us that this is a simple pie to make, "it goes together very quickly and very easily." Good news for those of us who plan to make it often!

Lois French
The Flavor & Spice of
Holy Cross Life
Holy Cross Parish
Batavia
ILLINOIS

1 Preheat the oven to 325°. Generously butter a 9-inch pie plate.

2 To make the Meringue Crust: With an electric mixer, beat the egg whites until frothy. Add the cream of tartar and continue beating while gradually adding the sugar and vanilla. Beat until the mixture forms stiff peaks.

3 Spread the mixture into the prepared pie plate, building up the edges higher than the center. Sprinkle with the slivered almonds.

4 Bake in the 325° oven for 40 minutes. Turn off the oven, leaving the door closed. Let the meringue remain in the oven for 1 hour. Remove from the oven; cool.

5 To make the Chocolate Filling: Melt the chocolate pieces over low heat, stirring constantly. Slowly stir in the boiling water; mix well. Set aside to cool.

6 In a medium bowl, beat the whipping cream until the mixture forms soft peaks. Gently fold the cooled chocolate mixture into the whipped cream. Spoon the mixture into the cooled crust. Cover and chill overnight.

TIPS FROM OUR KITCHEN

For greater volume, let the egg whites stand at room temperature about 30 minutes before beating them. As soon as the egg whites are foamy, start adding the sugar gradually, about *1 tablespoon* at a time. Start with medium speed on your electric mixer; switch to high speed when the whites become foamy. Stop beating when the mixture looks glossy and peaks stand straight when the beaters are lifted.

To make individual pies: Place a sheet of plain brown paper on the baking sheet. Draw eight 3-inch circles on the paper. Pipe the beaten egg white mixture through a pastry tube onto the circles, building the sides up to form shells. Or, use the back of a spoon to spread the beaten egg whites over the circles, building up the sides. Bake in a 300° oven for 35 minutes. Turn off the oven and let shells dry in the oven with the door closed for 1 hour.

Nutrition Analysis: (*Per Serving*): Calories: 169 / Cholesterol: 41 mg / Carbohydrates: 14 g / Protein: 2 g / Sodium: 32 mg / Fat: 12 g (Saturated Fat: 7 g) / Potassium: 60 mg.

PARTY CHOCOLATE PIE

PEANUT BUTTER PIE

PEANUT BUTTER PIE

Makes 6 to 8 Servings

Peanut Butter Mixture:
- ¾ cup sifted powdered sugar
- ½ cup crunchy peanut butter *or* smooth
- 1 9-inch pastry shell, baked

Filling:
- ¼ cup cornstarch
- ½ cup sugar
- ¼ teaspoon salt
- 2 cups milk, scalded
- 3 egg yolks
- 2 tablespoons butter *or* margarine

Meringue:
- 3 egg whites
- ½ teaspoon vanilla
- 3 tablespoons sugar

◆   ◆   ◆

Mrs. Fanning's aunts spent a great deal of time thinking of and preparing special dishes for their grandnieces and grandnephews. Fifteen years ago, these lovely ladies brought this pie and the recipe to Mrs. Fanning. The wise aunts knew it would become a Fanning family favorite. This is sure to be a hit in your home, too.

Mrs. Thomas Fanning

<u>Winning Seasons</u>

The Junior League of Tuscaloosa

Tuscaloosa

ALABAMA

1 Preheat the oven to 350°. To make the peanut butter mixture: In a medium bowl, cut the powdered sugar into the peanut butter until the mixture is well combined. Crumble *half* of the mixture into the bottom of the pastry shell.

2 To make the filling: Combine the cornstarch with the ½ cup sugar and the salt. Gradually stir in the scalded milk. In the top of a double boiler, beat the egg yolks until they are pale yellow. Slowly stir in the scalded milk mixture. Place the top of the double boiler over the bottom filled with boiling water. Cook, stirring, about 5 minutes or until the mixture is thickened and bubbly. Stir in the butter or margarine and vanilla. Remove from the heat. Wash the beaters.

3 To make the meringue: In a large mixing bowl, beat the egg whites until foamy. Gradually add the 3 tablespoons sugar, beating until stiff peaks form (tips stand straight).

4 Pour the hot filling over the peanut butter mixture in the pastry shell.

5 Spoon the meringue over the filling, first around the edges to seal the crust, then spreading toward the center to prevent shrinkage of the meringue during baking.

6 Crumble the reserved peanut butter mixture over the meringue.

7 Bake in the 350° oven about 15 minutes or until the meringue is lightly browned. Place on a wire rack and allow to cool 1 hour, then refrigerate.

TIPS FROM OUR KITCHEN

If you don't own a double boiler, don't scald the milk. In place of Step 2: In a medium saucepan, combine the ½ cup sugar, cornstarch, and salt. Gradually stir in the milk. Cook and stir over medium-high heat until the mixture is thickened and bubbly. Reduce the heat; cook and stir for 2 minutes more. Remove the saucepan from the heat. Beat the yolks lightly with a fork. Gradually stir about *1 cup* of the hot filling into the yolks. Return all of the hot filling to the saucepan and bring to a gentle boil. Cook and stir for 2 minutes more. Remove the saucepan from the heat and stir in the butter or margarine and vanilla.

Nutrition Analysis (*Per Serving*): Calories: 433 / Cholesterol: 92 mg / Carbohydrates: 50 g / Protein: 10 g / Sodium: 294 mg / Fat: 23 g (Saturated Fat: 7 g) / Potassium: 252 mg.

Makes 8 Servings
Crust:
1¼	cups all-purpose flour
¼	teaspoon salt
⅓	cup shortening *or* lard
3 to 4	tablespoons cold water

Filling:
4	eggs
1	cup sugar
1	cup chopped pecans
1	cup dark *or* light corn syrup
⅓	cup melted butter *or* margarine
1	teaspoon vanilla
⅛	teaspoon salt

♦ ♦ ♦

Ann Ackenbach and her husband have moved all over the country. As they moved, Ann built up her recipe collection, gathering favorites from friends and neighbors. With all of the different recipe sources, Ann has a "collection of memories as well as a collection of recipes."

Ann Ackenbach
Madonna Heights Ladies
Auxiliary Favorite Recipe
Collections
Madonna Heights Ladies
Auxiliary
Huntington
NEW YORK

1 Preheat the oven to 450°. To make the crust: In a medium bowl, stir together the flour and the ¼ teaspoon salt. Using a pastry blender, cut in the shortening or lard until the pieces are the size of small peas.

2 Sprinkle *1 tablespoon* of the cold water over part of the mixture; gently toss with a fork. Push to the side of the bowl. Repeat until all of the dough is moistened. Form the dough into a ball.

3 On a lightly floured surface, flatten the dough with your hands. Using a rolling pin, roll the dough from the center to the edges, forming a circle about 12 inches in diameter. Wrap the pastry around the rolling pin; unroll onto a 9-inch pie plate. Ease the pastry into the pie plate, being careful not to stretch the pastry. Trim to ½ inch beyond the edge of the pie plate; fold under and flute the edge high.

4 Bake in the 450° oven for 10 to 12 minutes or until golden. Cool on a wire rack. Reduce the oven temperature to 350°.

5 To make the filling: In a large mixing bowl, beat the eggs with an electric mixer on medium speed about 1 minute or until the eggs are light and fluffy. Add the sugar and beat for 1 minute more. Using a wooden spoon, stir in the pecans, dark or light corn syrup, melted butter or margarine, vanilla and the ⅛ teaspoon salt; mix thoroughly.

6 Pour the filling into the pastry-lined pie plate.

7 Bake the pie in the 350° oven about 50 minutes or until a knife inserted near the center comes out clean. Remove the pie from the oven and cool on a wire rack.

 TIPS FROM OUR KITCHEN

To make a decorative edge on your pastry shell, trim the pastry to the edge of the pie plate. Roll out the pastry scraps until very thin. Using a canapé cutter or knife, cut the pastry into desired shapes. Brush the edge of the pastry shell with *melted butter* or *margarine*. Arrange the cutouts on the edge of the pastry shell and press lightly to secure.

Nutrition Analysis (*Per Serving*): Calories: 548 / Cholesterol: 127 mg / Carbohydrates: 71 g / Protein: 6 g / Sodium: 239 mg / Fat: 28 g (Saturated Fat: 8 g) / Potassium: 107 mg.

GEORGIA'S PECAN PIE

LEMON LUSCIOUS PIE

LEMON LUSCIOUS PIE

Makes 8 Servings

1	cup sugar
3	tablespoons cornstarch
1	tablespoon grated lemon peel
¼	cup lemon juice
3	egg yolks
1	cup milk
¼	cup butter *or* margarine, cut up
1	cup dairy sour cream
1	9-inch pie shell, baked
1	cup whipping cream
2	tablespoons sugar
1	teaspoon vanilla

◆   ◆   ◆

Lucy Di Meglio tells us that she received this recipe for Lemon Luscious Pie from an old friend who was an excellent baker. Lucy is fortunate enough to have a large lemon tree in her backyard, and she believes that the combination of a homemade crust and fresh lemons gives her pies an extra-special touch.

Lucy Di Meglio
Around the World,
Around Our Town:
Recipes from San Pedro
Friends of San Pedro Library
San Pedro
CALIFORNIA

1 In a medium saucepan, combine the 1 cup sugar, the cornstarch and lemon peel. Stir in the lemon juice, egg yolks and milk until blended. Add the butter or margarine.

2 Cook the mixture over medium heat, stirring constantly until thickened and bubbly. Cook and stir for 2 minutes more. Cover the surface of the filling with plastic wrap and refrigerate for 30 minutes.

3 Remove the filling from the refrigerator. Fold in the sour cream. Spoon the filling into the pie shell. Cover the surface of the pie with plastic wrap and refrigerate for at least 2 hours.

4 In a small mixing bowl, beat the whipping cream with an electric mixer until thickened. Gradually beat in the 2 tablespoons sugar and the vanilla. Continue to beat until the whipped cream is fluffy. Spread the whipped cream over the top of the pie. Refrigerate for 1 to 2 hours.

TIPS FROM OUR KITCHEN

You'll need to buy one large or two medium lemons to have enough juice and peel for this recipe. Look for well-shaped fruits with smooth, evenly yellow skin.

For best results when whipping the cream, chill the bowl and the beaters in your freezer for 10 minutes before you begin. Be sure that your cream is very cold and whip it with an electric mixer

set on medium speed (not high) to avoid overbeating. (Overbeating will cause your cream to turn into butter.) When choosing your bowl, keep in mind that whipping cream doubles in volume when whipped.

To make a decorative edge on your pastry shell, roll out the pastry scraps until very thin. Use a knife or canapé cutter to cut the pastry into desired shapes. Brush the edge of the pastry shell with water. Arrange the cutouts on the edge of the pastry shell and press lightly to secure.

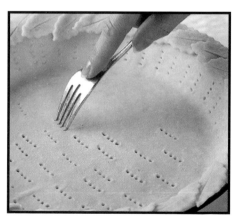

To prevent the crust from bubbling too much or shrinking while baking, use the tines of a fork to prick the unbaked pastry shell several times. Be sure to prick the bottom and the side.

Nutrition Analysis (*Per Serving*): Calories: 510 / Cholesterol: 151 mg / Carbohydrates: 48 g / Protein: 6 g / Sodium: 172 mg / Fat: 34 g (Saturated Fat: 17 g) / Potassium: 147 mg.

FUDGE SUNDAE PIE

Makes 8 Servings
- ¼ cup light corn syrup
- 3 tablespoons margarine *or* butter
- 2 tablespoons brown sugar
- 2½ cups crisp rice cereal
- ¼ cup peanut butter
- ¼ cup fudge ice cream sauce
- 3 tablespoons light corn syrup
- 1 quart vanilla ice cream

Milk

♦ ♦ ♦

Joyce Terryberry told us that she usually likes simple recipes and that her children like helping her with them. Joyce makes Fudge Sundae Pie often because it's quick, easy and her children love the taste and the preparation. Occasionally Joyce uses this fast, delicious pie when she's entertaining. She recommends allowing Fudge Sundae Pie to thaw about five minutes before serving for easier cutting.

Joyce Terryberry
101 Years of Treasured Recipes
United Methodist Women
Imperial
NEBRASKA

1 In a small saucepan, combine the ¼ cup light corn syrup, the margarine or butter and brown sugar. Cook and stir over medium heat until the margarine or butter melts. Combine the rice cereal and the syrup mixture, stirring until the cereal is well coated.

2 Using the back of a spoon, evenly press the cereal mixture over the bottom and up the sides of a 9-inch pie plate to form the pie crust; freeze about 10 minutes or until set.

3 Meanwhile, in a small bowl, stir together the peanut butter, fudge sauce and the 3 tablespoons light corn syrup. Spread *half* of the peanut butter mixture over the bottom of the cereal crust.

4 Stir the vanilla ice cream to soften it slightly. Spoon the vanilla ice cream over the peanut butter layer, spreading it evenly. Drizzle the remaining peanut butter mixture over the ice cream; if the peanut butter mixture becomes too stiff to drizzle, stir in a few drops of the milk.

5 Freeze the pie until firm.

 TIPS FROM OUR KITCHEN

If you'd like more peanut flavor, add ¼ cup of chopped peanuts to the crust mixture.

Substitute chocolate or butter brickle ice cream for the vanilla ice cream in this recipe. Or, for a lower-fat treat, use ice milk or low-fat frozen yogurt instead of the vanilla ice cream.

The best way to soften the ice cream is to place it in a chilled bowl and stir it with a wooden spoon until softened.

For easier serving, set the frozen pie on a warm towel to help thaw and loosen the bottom crust.

If desired, sprinkle the top of the pie with chopped peanuts, cashews or pecans before serving. Or, garnish each serving with a swirl of whipped cream and a maraschino cherry.

Nutrition Analysis (*Per Serving*): Calories: 352 / Cholesterol: 30 mg / Carbohydrates: 47 g / Protein: 6 g / Sodium: 232 mg / Fat: 17 g (Saturated Fat: 7 g) / Potassium: 235 mg.

FUDGE SUNDAE PIE

BANANA SPLIT

BANANA SPLIT

Makes 15 to 16 Servings
Crust:
- 2 cups graham cracker crumbs (28 crackers)
- ½ cup margarine *or* butter, melted

Filling:
- 2 cups sifted powdered sugar
- 1 8-ounce package cream cheese, softened
- 1 8-ounce container frozen whipped dessert topping, thawed
- 4 large bananas
- 1 20-ounce can crushed pineapple, drained
- 1 21-ounce can cherry pie filling
- 1 cup chopped pecans (optional)

❖   ❖   ❖

Banana Split is a treat that is loved by Betty Brannan's three children and now her grand-children. Betty said that this dessert is a great time-saver and "not only delicious, but easy to make." When she heard that Banana Split was going to be included in this cooking series, she said that the news was the "highlight of my week."

Betty Brannan
Between Greene Leaves
Greene County Homemakers
Association
Carrollton
ILLINOIS

1 To make the crust: In a large bowl, stir together the graham cracker crumbs and melted margarine or butter. Firmly press the cracker-margarine mixture into the bottom of a 13x9x2-inch baking pan; chill the crust.

2 To make the filling: In a large mixing bowl, beat the powdered sugar and cream cheese with an electric mixer until combined. Carefully fold *half* of the whipped dessert topping into the mixture.

3 Spread the filling on top of the chilled crust; set aside.

4 Slice the bananas; arrange on top of the filling. Top with the crushed pineapple. Then, cover the pineapple layer with the cherry pie filling. Cover and refrigerate the dessert for 4 to 8 hours.

5 Garnish each serving with the remaining whipped dessert topping and sprinkle with the pecans, if desired.

 TIPS FROM OUR KITCHEN

Sift the powdered sugar before measuring it. If you don't have a sifter, place a wire sieve over a mixing bowl. Add the powdered sugar and press it against the sides of the sieve with a spoon.

You can substitute almonds for the pecans in this recipe. If desired, you can toast the pecans or almonds. To toast: Spread the pecans or almonds in a shallow baking pan; toast in a 350° oven for 5 to 10 minutes or until light golden brown, stirring once or twice.

For a lower-calorie version of this dessert, substitute Neufchatel for the cream cheese and use "lite" whipped topping and pie filling.

If you prefer chocolate in your banana split, you have a few choices. You can substitute chocolate whipped topping and/or garnish each serving with chocolate curls. Or, you can drizzle the banana split with chocolate topping.

If desired, substitute peach or strawberry pie filling for the cherry pie filling in this recipe.

Nutrition Analysis (*Per Serving*): Calories: 350 / Cholesterol: 17 mg / Carbohydrates: 52 g / Protein: 3 g / Sodium: 187 mg / Fat: 16 g (Saturated Fat: 5 g) / Potassium: 286 mg.

PEACH MELBA PIE

Makes 8 Servings

   2⅔ cups flaked coconut
       (7 ounces)
    1 cup finely chopped walnuts
    ¼ cup butter *or* margarine,
       melted
    1 quart peach ice cream,
       softened
    1 pint vanilla ice cream,
       softened
    1 12-ounce package frozen
       loose-pack raspberries,
       thawed
    ⅓ cup sugar
    1 tablespoon cornstarch
    1 cup sliced, peeled peaches

♦   ♦   ♦

Clara Catliota's daughter, Carolyn Brigham, gave her the recipe for this refreshing dessert. When asked about its source, Carolyn explained, "In Cleveland, we were part of a group of six couples who got together once a month for meals." At one of these gatherings, Carolyn first tasted her friend's Peach Melba Pie, which has since become a family favorite.

Clara Catliota
Plum Good
The Christ Child Society of Cleveland
Chagrin Falls
OHIO

1 Preheat the oven to 325°.

2 In a medium mixing bowl, stir together the coconut, walnuts and melted butter or margarine. Using the back of a spoon, press the mixture into the bottom and up the sides of an ungreased 10-inch pie plate.

3 Bake in the 325° oven for 10 to 15 minutes or until the crust is golden brown; cool.

4 Spread the softened peach ice cream in the cooled pie shell. Cover and freeze the pie for 1 to 2 hours or until firm. Spread the softened vanilla ice cream over the peach ice cream. Cover and freeze for 1 to 2 hours more or until firm.

5 Drain the raspberries, reserving the juice. In a small saucepan, combine the sugar and cornstarch. Stir in the raspberry juice.

6 Cook and stir the juice mixture over medium heat until the mixture is thickened and bubbly. Cook and stir for 2 minutes more. Stir in the raspberries. Cover and cool.

7 To serve, cut the pie into wedges. Drizzle with the raspberry sauce and garnish with the peach slices.

TIPS FROM OUR KITCHEN

This amount fills a 10-inch pie plate. If you have only a 9-inch size, you'll want to use less crust and ice cream.

To soften the ice cream: Place it in a mixing bowl. Use a spoon to stir and press it against the side of the bowl until it is pliable. If the ice cream starts to melt, return the bowl to the freezer until it becomes firm.

To simplify serving, set the frozen pie on a warm cloth to help loosen the bottom crust. Dip the knife in water after each cut.

Frozen peach and vanilla yogurts also can be used in this recipe. Or, experiment with other fruit-flavored ice creams and yogurts.

Frozen ice-cream pies like this one can be stored in freezer bags in the freezer up to 2 weeks.

Nutrition Analysis (*Per Serving*): Calories: 528 / Cholesterol: 60 mg / Carbohydrates: 54 g / Protein: 7 g / Sodium: 152 mg / Fat: 34 g (Saturated Fat: 18 g) / Potassium: 457 mg.

PEACH MELBA PIE

FRUIT TART

FRUIT TART

Makes 10 to 12 Servings

2   cups all-purpose flour
½   cup granulated sugar
1   teaspoon baking powder
½   cup margarine *or* butter
1   egg
2   tablespoons water
¾   cup packed brown sugar
3   tablespoons all-purpose flour
      (⅓ cup if using pears)
1   teaspoon ground cinnamon
3   pounds baking apples *or*
      pears, peeled, cored and sliced
1   tablespoon margarine *or*
      butter

◆   ◆   ◆

Marlene Riley's Fruit Tart has been handed down through her family for generations; her mother and her grandmother made the dessert when she was a child, and now Marlene's grown children make Fruit Tart, too. When Marlene's favorite fruits come into season, she makes about a dozen or so tarts and then freezes them so that she can serve them whenever she likes.

Marlene Riley
Stanford University Medical
Center Auxiliary Cookbook
Stanford University Medical
Center Auxiliary
Stanford
CALIFORNIA

1 Preheat the oven to 350°. Grease a 9-inch springform pan; set aside.

2 In a large bowl, stir together the 2 cups flour, the granulated sugar and baking powder. Using a pastry blender or 2 knives, cut in the ½ cup margarine or butter until the mixture forms crumbs that are the size of small peas.

3 In a small bowl, stir together the egg and water. Gradually add the egg mixture to the flour mixture, tossing with a fork just until the ingredients are moistened.

4 Press the pastry dough over the bottom and 2 inches up the sides of the prepared pan.

5 In a very large bowl, stir together the brown sugar, the 2 tablespoons flour and the cinnamon. Add the apple or pear slices. Toss to coat the slices with the brown sugar mixture.

6 Place the fruit mixture in the pastry-lined pan. Dot the fruit with the 1 tablespoon margarine or butter. Cover the pan with aluminum foil and bake in the 350° oven for 50 minutes (45 minutes if using pears). Remove the aluminum foil and bake about 20 minutes more or until the fruit is tender.

7 Set the pan on a wire rack and let the tart cool slightly. Carefully remove the sides of the pan. Cool the tart before serving.

 TIPS FROM OUR KITCHEN

If desired, add chopped nuts or a crumb topping to the filled tart before baking. One possible topping is made with ¾ cup finely crushed *vanilla wafers* (about 20), ½ cup chopped *almonds* and 3 tablespoons *melted margarine* or *butter.*

When you cover the fruit tart for the first part of baking, simply lay a square piece of aluminum foil over the top of the pan; the aluminum foil doesn't need to be crimped to the pan edges.

Fruit tarts such as this one can be kept safely at room temperature for 1 day, but afterwards leftovers should be refrigerated.

Nutrition Analysis (*Per Serving*): Calories: 377 / Cholesterol: 21 mg / Carbohydrates: 65 g / Protein: 4 g / Sodium: 147 mg / Fat: 13 g (Saturated Fat: 2 g) / Potassium: 251 mg.

FOR THE GLORY PIE

Makes 8 Servings

1	9-inch unbaked pie shell
¾ to 1	cup sugar
1	8-ounce carton dairy sour cream
3	tablespoons all-purpose flour
¼	teaspoon salt
4	cups fresh blackberries
¼	cup fine dry bread crumbs
2	tablespoons sugar
1	tablespoon butter *or* margarine, melted

◆ ◆ ◆

When Huberta Young Manning moved into her new home about eight years ago, she found a patch of blackberries in her yard and began looking for recipes to use the berries. Her search resulted in the discovery of this delicious recipe for For the Glory Pie. Huberta tells us that she makes the pie every year during blackberry season and "always on the Fourth of July." She also freezes some of the fresh blackberries to enjoy throughout the year.

Huberta Young Manning
<u>**Cookin' with the Lion**</u>
Penn State Alumni Association
University Park
PENNSYLVANIA

1 Preheat the oven to 450°.

2 Line the bottom of a pastry-lined 9-inch pie plate with a double thickness of foil. Bake in the 450° oven for 5 minutes. Remove the foil and bake for 5 minutes more. Remove the pie shell from the oven and cool slightly. Reduce the oven temperature to 375°.

3 Meanwhile, in a small bowl, stir together the ¾ to 1 cup sugar, the sour cream, flour and salt until combined. Set aside.

4 Place the blackberries in the pre-baked pastry shell. Spread the sour cream mixture evenly over the berries.

5 In a small bowl, stir together the bread crumbs, the 2 tablespoons sugar and the melted butter or margarine. Sprinkle the bread crumb mixture on top of the sour cream mixture.

6 Cover the edge of the pie with foil and bake in the 375° oven for 25 minutes. Remove the foil. Bake for 20 to 25 minutes more or until the top of the pie is golden and the berry mixture bubbles slightly.

 TIPS FROM OUR KITCHEN

Use fresh blackberries for this recipe; frozen berries don't work well because they release too much juice as they thaw. However, you could substitute other fresh berries like blueberries or raspberries.

Fine dry bread crumbs are easy to make. For ¼ cup of crumbs, place one slice of dried or lightly toasted bread in a plastic bag and crush it with a rolling pin.

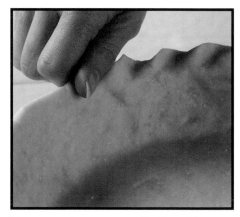

Pie crust edges are usually fluted by pressing the dough with the forefinger of one hand against the thumb and forefinger of the other hand. To make a rope-shaped edge, press the dough between the thumb and a bent forefinger.

An easy way to cover just the edge of the pie with foil is to cut a large circle out of the center of a 12-inch square of foil.

Nutrition Analysis (*Per Serving*): Calories: 353 / Cholesterol: 17 mg / Carbohydrates: 50 g / Protein: 4 g / Sodium: 187 mg / Fat: 17 g (Saturated Fat: 7 g) / Potassium: 210 mg.

FOR THE GLORY PIE

GRAMMY'S RHUBARB CREAM PIE

GRAMMY'S RHUBARB CREAM PIE

Makes 8 Servings
- 3 cups chopped rhubarb
- 1 unbaked 9-inch pie shell with edges crimped high
- 1 cup sugar
- ¼ cup all-purpose flour
- 1½ cups milk
- 3 egg yolks, beaten
- 1 teaspoon vanilla

Meringue:
- 3 egg whites
- ¼ teaspoon cream of tartar
- ⅓ cup sugar

❖ ❖ ❖

Exclusively Rhubarb was inspired by a rhubarb cake recipe. At first there was some concern about finding sufficient recipes to justify an entire cookbook. The fears were unfounded, however, and the cookbook of well over 250 rhubarb recipes was a success. In its first edition, the cookbook sold 7,000 copies, generating over $15,000. Initially, Exclusively Rhubarb was created to raise funds for the Covenant Soup Kitchen. Currently, proceeds benefit the Coventry Historical Society.

Dale Schimmel
Exclusively Rhubarb
The Coventry Historical Society
Coventry
CONNECTICUT

1 Preheat the oven to 350°.

2 Place the rhubarb in a 1-quart casserole. *Do not add water.* Cover and bake in the 350° oven about 30 minutes or until the rhubarb is soft, but not mushy. Remove the rhubarb from the oven; drain. Cool the rhubarb and spread it into the unbaked pie shell. Increase oven temperature to 450°.

3 In a small bowl, stir together the 1 cup sugar and the flour. Stir in the milk, beaten egg yolks and vanilla until well mixed. Pour the mixture over the rhubarb in the pie shell.

4 Cover the edge of the pie shell with foil. Bake in the 450° oven for 15 minutes. Reduce heat to 350° and bake for 30 minutes. Remove the foil and bake about 15 minutes more or until the filling is set and a knife inserted near the center comes out clean.

5 Meanwhile, to prepare the meringue: In a medium mixing bowl, beat the egg whites and cream of tartar with an electric mixer on medium speed about 1 minute or until soft peaks form (tips curl). Gradually add the ⅓ cup sugar, *1 tablespoon* at a time, beating on high speed about 4 minutes more or until the mixture forms stiff, glossy peaks (tips stand straight) and the sugar is nearly dissolved.

6 Spread the meringue over the hot filling, carefully sealing to the edge of the pastry. Bake in the 350° oven for 15 minutes. Remove the pie from the oven and cool on a wire rack. Cover and chill until ready to serve.

 TIPS FROM OUR KITCHEN

Use a foil ring to help keep the pie edges from burning. To make a foil ring: Fold a 12-inch foil square into quarters; cut out the center, leaving a 7½-inch hole in the foil. Unfold and mold loosely over the pie edges.

Nutrition Analysis (*Per Serving*): Calories: 337 / Cholesterol: 83 mg / Carbohydrates: 53 g / Protein: 7 g / Sodium: 116 mg / Fat: 12 g (Saturated Fat: 3 g) / Potassium: 253 mg.

FRESH BLUEBERRY PIE

Makes 8 Servings
- 1 cup sugar
- 3 tablespoons quick-cooking tapioca
- ¼ teaspoon salt
- 4 cups fresh blueberries
- 1 tablespoon lemon juice
- Pastry for a double-crust 9-inch pie
- All-purpose flour
- 1 tablespoon margarine *or* butter
- Milk
- Sugar

◆　　◆　　◆

Pies are Mary Helen Maddigan's favorite dessert. This recipe evolved from one of Mary Helen's fruit pie recipes. Every year during blueberry season, Mary Helen stocks up on the berries and stores them in her freezer so that she can make this fresh dessert whenever she likes. When we asked if this is her favorite, Mary Helen told us that "it's a toss-up between this and cherry pie."

Mary Helen Maddigan
<u>*Culinary Compositions*</u>
The Keynotes of Music for Mt. Lebanon
Mt. Lebanon
PENNSYLVANIA

1 Preheat the oven to 375°.

2 In a large bowl, stir together the 1 cup sugar, the tapioca and salt. Add the blueberries and lemon juice. Using a wooden spoon, gently toss the blueberry mixture until the ingredients are well mixed; set aside.

3 Roll out *half* of the pastry into an 11-inch circle on a lightly floured pastry cloth or piece of waxed paper.

4 Wrap the pastry around the rolling pin by lifting the pastry cloth onto the rolling pin; the pastry should slide easily onto the pin. Then slowly roll the pin to wrap the pastry around it. Loosely unroll the pastry onto the pie plate, being careful not to stretch the dough. To repair any tears in the pastry, moisten the edges with a little *water* and press together. Trim the pastry even with the rim of the pie plate.

5 Spoon the blueberry mixture into the pastry-lined pie plate. Dot the top of the blueberry filling with the margarine or butter.

6 Roll out the remaining pastry into a 12-inch circle on the pastry cloth or

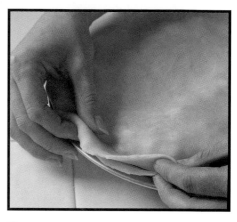

waxed paper. Follow Step 4 to transfer the pastry and place it over the filled crust. Trim the top crust ½ inch beyond the edge of the plate.

7 Fold the top crust under the bottom crust; flute the edge. Cut several vents in the top crust. Brush the top crust with the milk and sprinkle with the additional sugar.

8 Bake the pie in the 375° oven for 45 to 50 minutes or until the crust is golden brown. If necessary, cover the edge of the crust with aluminum foil to prevent overbrowning.

 TIPS FROM OUR KITCHEN

Tapioca is a starch extracted from the roots of the tropical cassava plant. Quick-cooking tapioca is a good choice for pie thickening because it becomes clear during cooking. Unlike cornstarch- and flour-thickened mixtures, tapioca-thickened mixtures retain their thickness after being frozen.

Nutrition Analysis (*Per Serving*): Calories: 425 / Cholesterol: 0 mg / Carbohydrates: 62 g / Protein: 4 g / Sodium: 223 mg / Fat: 19 g (Saturated Fat: 5 g) / Potassium: 102 mg.

FRESH BLUEBERRY PIE

DEEP-DISH PUMPKIN PIE

DEEP-DISH PUMPKIN PIE

Makes 8 to 10 Servings
1¼ cups all-purpose flour
¼ cup packed brown sugar
¼ cup granulated sugar
⅔ cup cold margarine *or* butter, cut into small pieces
⅔ cup chopped pecans, walnuts *or* macadamia nuts
1 16-ounce can pumpkin
1 14-ounce can sweetened condensed milk
2 eggs, beaten
1 teaspoon ground cinnamon
½ teaspoon ground allspice
½ teaspoon salt
Vanilla ice cream *or* whipped cream (optional)

♦   ♦   ♦

Jeanne Morascini remembers always loving to cook, and she credits her father. Jeanne lived with her mother and spent summers with her father when she was young. Her dad was always in the kitchen, and he owned a restaurant. As a result, Jeanne likes experimenting in the kitchen and creating her own recipes.

Jeanne Morascini
Exclusively Pumpkin
The Coventry Historical Society, Inc.
Coventry
CONNECTICUT

1 Preheat the oven to 350°.

2 In a medium bowl, stir together the flour, brown sugar and granulated sugar. Using a pastry blender or 2 knives, cut in the cold margarine or butter pieces until the mixture resembles fine crumbs. Stir in the pecans, walnuts or macadamia nuts.

3 Set aside *1 cup* of the crumb mixture. Firmly press the remaining crumb mixture over the bottom and halfway up the sides of a 2-quart rectangular baking dish; set aside.

4 In a large bowl, stir together the pumpkin, condensed milk, beaten eggs, cinnamon, allspice and salt until well mixed. Pour the mixture into the prepared baking dish. Sprinkle with the reserved crumb mixture.

5 Bake in the 350° oven about 55 minutes or until the topping is golden brown and the filling is set; cool. If desired, serve with the vanilla ice cream or whipped cream.

 TIPS FROM OUR KITCHEN

Sweetened condensed milk is cream colored, smooth, thick and sticky. It has no substitute, nor should it be used as a substitute for evaporated milk in other recipes.

Even though allspice tastes like a combination of cloves, cinnamon and nutmeg, actually it is a single berry. You can buy allspice either ground or whole. If you don't have allspice, try adding ⅛ to ¼ teaspoon *each* of ground cloves and ground nutmeg to the 1 teaspoon ground cinnamon in this recipe.

Nutrition Analysis (*Per Serving*): Calories: 505 / Cholesterol: 70 mg / Carbohydrates: 59 g / Protein: 9 g / Sodium: 396 mg / Fat: 27 g (Saturated Fat: 7 g) / Potassium: 401 mg.

APPLE BROWN BETTY

Makes 8 to 10 Servings

6 to 7	medium tart apples, peeled and thinly sliced (6 to 7 cups)
½	cup granulated sugar
¼	teaspoon lemon juice
⅛	teaspoon ground cinnamon
1	cup all-purpose flour
½	cup butter *or* margarine, softened
½	cup packed brown sugar
2	tablespoons granulated sugar
¼	teaspoon ground cinnamon
Vanilla ice cream *or* whipped cream	

◆   ◆   ◆

Linda Kaplan's mom, Mary Stone, treated the family to Apple Brown Betty fairly often when Linda was growing up. Linda said that even though Mary's in her late eighties, she still makes Bettys! An old family recipe, Apple Brown Betty dates back to the early 1900s and continues to pass from generation to generation: Linda said that her three-year-old granddaughter is beginning to help out when Brown Bettys are bakin'!

Linda Kaplan
Gracious Goodness
The Taste of Memphis
Memphis Symphony League
Memphis
TENNESSEE

1 Preheat the oven to 400°.

2 In a large bowl, stir together the apples, the ½ cup granulated sugar, the lemon juice and the ⅛ teaspoon cinnamon. Mix thoroughly. Spread the mixture into a 2-quart square baking dish; set aside.

3 In a medium bowl, stir together the flour and softened butter or margarine. Add the brown sugar, the 2 tablespoons granulated sugar and the ¼ teaspoon cinnamon, stirring until combined. Crumble the sugar-cinnamon mixture over the apple mixture.

4 Bake in the 400° oven for 25 to 30 minutes or until the top is lightly browned and the apples are tender. Serve warm with the ice cream or whipped cream.

TIPS FROM OUR KITCHEN

Use medium-tart apples, such as Jonagold, Golden Delicious, Cortland, Empire, Jonathan, Newtown Pippin, Northern Spy, Rome Beauty, Stayman or York Imperial.

Because the apples are thinly sliced, you can leave the peel on. To save yourself some time, you can use your food processor to slice the apples since the appearance of the apple slices isn't important.

If desired, add ½ cup raisins to the filling and/or ¼ cup chopped nuts to the topping.

This recipe works equally well with sliced pears or peaches instead of the apples.

Nutrition Analysis (*Per Serving*): Calories: 456 / Cholesterol: 61 mg / Carbohydrates: 70 g / Protein: 4 g / Sodium: 180 mg / Fat: 19 g (Saturated Fat: 12 g) / Potassium: 295 mg.

APPLE BROWN BETTY

ANNE BYRD'S STRAWBERRY COBBLER

ANNE BYRD'S STRAWBERRY COBBLER

Makes 6 to 8 Servings

- 6 cups whole strawberries, hulled
- ⅓ cup granulated sugar
- 2 cups all-purpose flour
- ⅔ cup granulated sugar
- 2 teaspoons baking powder
- ¼ teaspoon baking soda
- ¼ teaspoon salt
- ¾ cup butter *or* margarine
- 1 cup buttermilk
- Sifted powdered sugar

◆　◆　◆

Anne Byrd is a food specialist for several cooking foundations. Roseanne Nichols was her assistant for a number of years, and together they developed this recipe. Roseanne remembers that they tried a number of fruits before they decided juicy fresh strawberries would be great. Roseanne also told us that at one time she had her own catering business and continues to enjoy cooking, especially baking breads and cakes.

Roseanne Nichols
Southern Elegance
Junior League of Gaston County
Gastonia
NORTH CAROLINA

1 Preheat the oven to 375°. Lightly grease a 3-quart rectangular baking dish; set aside.

2 Place the whole strawberries in the prepared baking dish. Sprinkle with the ⅓ cup granulated sugar; set aside.

3 Sift the flour into a large bowl. Stir in the ⅔ cup granulated sugar, the baking powder, baking soda and salt. Using a pastry blender or 2 knives, cut in the butter or margarine until the mixture is coarse and crumbly. Add the buttermilk; stir until the mixture is blended. Using a wooden spoon, beat about 30 seconds or until a very thick batter forms.

4 Dollop the batter over the strawberries. Using the back of a spoon, spread the batter over the strawberries in the dish; any holes in the batter will fill in while baking.

5 Bake in the 375° oven about 35 minutes or until the top of the cobbler is golden brown. Sprinkle with the sifted powdered sugar. Serve warm.

 TIPS FROM OUR KITCHEN

Other fruits or combinations of fruit can be substituted for the strawberries in this recipe. Try blueberries, rhubarb, sliced peaches or raspberries. If you are using frozen fruit, thaw and drain the fruit before using it.

If you don't have a pastry blender, you can use 2 table knives to cut in the butter. Hold 1 knife in each hand and draw the knives across each other.

Unlike some cobbler recipes, this recipe places the topping on *unheated* fruit.

Nutrition Analysis (*Per Serving*): Calories: 514 / Cholesterol: 62 mg / Carbohydrates: 73 g / Protein: 5 g / Sodium: 470 mg / Fat: 24 g (Saturated Fat: 14 g) / Potassium: 297 mg.

APPLE DESSERT PANCAKE

Makes 6 to 8 Servings
- 5 tablespoons sugar
- 1 teaspoon ground cinnamon
- 2 tablespoons butter *or* margarine
- 2 medium apples, peeled, cored and thinly sliced
- ⅓ cup all-purpose flour
- ¼ teaspoon baking powder
- ⅛ teaspoon salt
- 2 eggs, separated
- ⅓ cup milk
- Sour cream, whipped cream, vanilla ice cream *or* vanilla yogurt (optional)

❖   ❖   ❖

It took the Dallas SPCA about a year to put together their cookbook. When it was published, all of the volunteers who worked on it got together at the shelter to celebrate, and each made a dish from the cookbook. Proceeds from cookbook sales provide much-needed funds to care for the animals at the shelter, and the cookbook is an excellent source of delicious recipes for the SPCA's bake sales.

Joi Weffelmeyer
Dallas SPCA Cookbook
Dallas SPCA
Dallas
TEXAS

1 In a small bowl, combine *2 table-spoons* of the sugar with the ground cinnamon. Set aside.

2 In a 10-inch skillet, with an oven-safe handle, melt the butter or margarine. Swirl the skillet to coat the entire bottom with the melted butter or margarine. Sprinkle the cinnamon-sugar mixture evenly over the melted butter or margarine.

3 Add the apples, cover and cook over low heat for 5 minutes, stirring once. Remove from heat. Preheat the oven to 400°.

4 Meanwhile, in a medium mixing bowl, stir together the flour, baking powder, salt, egg yolks and milk. Beat with a whisk until smooth.

5 In another medium mixing bowl, using an electric mixer, beat the egg whites with the remaining sugar until soft peaks form (tips curl). Carefully fold the egg white mixture into the flour mixture.

6 Pour the batter over the apples in the skillet. Bake in the 400° oven, uncovered, for 10 to 15 minutes or until golden and puffed.

7 Remove the skillet from the oven. Loosen the edges of the pancake with a spatula. Invert a flat, round serving plate over the skillet. Hold the plate and the skillet together, then flip so that the plate is on the bottom. Lift the skillet away. Serve the Apple Dessert Pancake cut into wedges and topped with sour cream, whipped cream, vanilla ice cream or vanilla yogurt, if desired.

 TIPS FROM OUR KITCHEN

For this recipe, you need a skillet with a handle that can be placed in a 400° oven. Check carefully, because the handles of some ovenproof skillets cannot withstand temperatures over 350°.

For variety, you can substitute pear slices for the apple slices in this recipe.

Nutrition Analysis (*Per Serving*): Calories: 146 / Cholesterol: 82 mg / Carbohydrates: 21 g / Protein: 3 g / Sodium: 125 mg / Fat: 6 g (Saturated Fat: 3 g) / Potassium: 82 mg.

APPLE DESSERT PANCAKE

RONNIE'S MOM'S APPLE DUMPLINGS

RONNIE'S MOM'S APPLE DUMPLINGS

Makes 6 Servings

2	cups sugar
2	cups water
¼	teaspoon ground cinnamon
¼	teaspoon ground nutmeg
¼	cup butter *or* margarine
6	small apples
2	cups all-purpose flour
2	teaspoons baking powder
½	teaspoon salt
¾	cup shortening
½	cup milk
2	tablespoons sugar
¼	teaspoon ground cinnamon
⅛	teaspoon ground nutmeg
2	tablespoons butter *or* margarine, cut up

✦   ✦   ✦

"I truly believe that an apple a day keeps the doctor away," says Suzanne King. When she married Ronnie, he asked Suzanne to get the recipe for his mom's apple dumplings, which she happily did. Now it's a family tradition to make Ronnie's Mom's Apple Dumplings every fall.

Suzanne King
Bona Vista's Best Recipes
Bona Vista Rehabilitation Center
Kokomo
INDIANA

1 In a medium saucepan, stir together the 2 cups sugar, the water, the ¼ teaspoon cinnamon and the ¼ teaspoon nutmeg. Bring the mixture to a boil, then add the ¼ cup butter or margarine. Set aside.

2 Preheat the oven to 375°. Peel and core the apples. If desired, coarsely chop the apples or leave them whole.

3 In a large mixing bowl, stir together the flour, baking powder and salt. Using a pastry blender, cut the shortening into the flour mixture until the mixture resembles coarse crumbs. Add the milk all at once and stir until the flour mixture is just moistened. Form the dough into a ball.

4 On a lightly floured surface, roll the dough into a ¼-inch-thick rectangle. Cut the dough into six 5- or 6-inch squares. Place an equal portion of the chopped apple or a whole apple on each square.

5 Stir together the 2 tablespoons sugar, the ¼ teaspoon cinnamon and the ⅛ teaspoon nutmeg. Sprinkle a portion of the sugar mixture on each of the mounds of chopped apple or on the whole apple. Dot with the 2 tablespoons butter or margarine. For each dumpling, fold the corners of the dough to the center and pinch the edges together to seal.

6 Place the dumplings in a 13x9x2-inch baking pan. Pour the syrup over all. Bake in the 375° oven about 35 minutes or until the apples are tender and pastry is golden. Serve warm.

 TIPS FROM OUR KITCHEN

Baking apples and all-purpose apples are the best choices for the dumplings.

The dumplings are taller when whole apples are used and flatter when chopped apples are used.

Don't be concerned by the thin consistency of the syrup; it thickens during baking.

Nutrition Analysis (*Per Serving*): Calories: 799 / Cholesterol: 32 mg / Carbohydrates: 113 g / Protein: 5 g / Sodium: 328 mg / Fat: 38 g (Saturated Fat: 14 g) / Potassium: 161 mg.

LEMON CUPS

Makes 8 Servings

- 1 cup sugar
- ¼ cup all-purpose flour
- 2 tablespoons butter *or* margarine, melted
- Pinch of salt
- 1 teaspoon grated lemon peel
- ⅓ cup lemon juice
- 3 egg yolks, slightly beaten
- 1½ cups milk
- 3 egg whites, beaten to stiff peaks
- ½ cup whipping cream, whipped

♦ ♦ ♦

The recipe for Lemon Cups has been in Nancy Spivey's family for a very long time. Nancy's mother gave her this family-favorite recipe, and Nancy began making the dessert shortly after she married. She and her family enjoy Lemon Cups after a big meal, and especially during the summer. "In fact, whenever I need a dessert, this one comes to mind immediately."

Nancy Spivey
Market to Market
The Hickory Service League of N.C., Inc.
Hickory
NORTH CAROLINA

1 Preheat the oven to 350°. Grease eight 6-ounce custard cups; set aside.

2 In a large mixing bowl, using an electric mixer, beat together the sugar, flour, melted butter or margarine and salt. Add the lemon peel and lemon juice; stir. Set aside.

3 Stir together the slightly beaten egg yolks and the milk. Add the egg yolk mixture to the creamed mixture; stir until well mixed.

4 Using a wire wisk, carefully fold in the stiffly beaten egg whites.

5 Pour the mixture into the prepared custard cups. Place the filled custard cups in a 13x9x2-inch baking pan, a roasting pan or a broiler pan without the rack. Place the pan on the oven rack. Carefully add hot water to the pan to a 1-inch depth.

6 Bake in the 350° oven for 35 to 40 minutes or until golden and the tops spring back when lightly touched. When done, each dessert will have custard on the bottom and cake on the top. Serve warm or chilled. Top with the whipped cream.

TIPS FROM OUR KITCHEN

For a fancy presentation, pipe the whipped cream in a lattice pattern on each dessert. Do this by using a pastry or decorating bag fitted with a small star tip. Top the whipped cream with a lemon peel curl, if you wish.

If desired, bake this as one cake in a 2-quart square baking dish for 35 to 40 minutes or until golden and the top springs back when lightly touched.

You'll need 2 medium lemons to get ⅓ cup of fresh juice.

Nutrition Analysis (*Per Serving*): Calories: 239 / Cholesterol: 111 mg / Carbohydrates: 31 g / Protein: 5 g / Sodium: 98 mg / Fat: 11 g (Saturated Fat: 6 g) / Potassium: 124 mg.

LEMON CUPS

JUL GROT

JUL GROT

Makes 12 Servings
- 1 cup long-grain rice
- 1 teaspoon salt
- 2 quarts milk
- 2 2-inch pieces cinnamon stick
- ½ cup sugar
- 1 tablespoon butter *or* margarine
- Ground cinnamon (optional)
- Sugar (optional)
- Raisins (optional)

◆　◆　◆

Elna Dorothea Ingabourg Johanson Duncan's father immigrated from Sweden through Canada, eventually settling in New Sweden, Maine. Elna's mother also settled in New Sweden. She brought with her this recipe for Jul Grot that had been given to her by her mother in Sweden. We imagine the delicious holiday dessert was quite popular in the settlement, as we're sure it will be in your home.

Elna Duncan
(Jean Waters's mother)
Country Living Cookbook
Waterloo Area Historical Society
Stockbridge
MICHIGAN

1 Place the rice and salt in a heavy 3-quart saucepan. Add *4 cups* of the milk and the cinnamon sticks. Bring to boiling. Reduce heat and cook over low heat, uncovered, for 30 minutes, stirring occasionally with a wooden spoon. Gradually add the remaining milk.

2 Continue to cook about 30 minutes more or until the rice is tender. Add the ½ cup sugar and cook 5 minutes more.

3 Remove the saucepan from the heat. Remove the cinnamon sticks from the mixture and discard. Add the butter and stir until it has melted.

4 Pour the pudding into a warm serving dish or individual dishes. If desired, sprinkle with the ground cinnamon, sugar and raisins.

TIPS FROM OUR KITCHEN

For the best consistency, allow the pudding to stand about an hour before garnishing and serving.

Swedish tradition calls for adding a whole almond to the pudding. Legend has it that the person who finds the almond in his or her serving will be married within a year. Secretly slip in the almond just before serving the pudding and see what happens.

A garnish of whipped cream and fresh strawberries helps to give this dish a festive flair. Or you may prefer to imitate the people of Finland and top it with a thickened fruit juice sauce.

Nutrition Analysis *(Per Serving)*: Calories: 176 / Cholesterol: 15 mg / Carbohydrates: 28 g / Protein: 7 g / Sodium: 270 mg / Fat: 4 g (Saturated Fat: 3 g) / Potassium: 270 mg.

TRADITIONAL BREAD PUDDING

Makes 12 to 15 Servings

Custard Sauce:
- 4 eggs, beaten
- 1½ cups milk
- ⅔ cup granulated sugar
- 1 teaspoon vanilla

Hard Sauce:
- ½ cup butter *or* margarine
- 2 cups sifted powdered sugar
- 2 teaspoons vanilla

Bread Pudding:
- 8 cups dry bread cubes
- 1 cup raisins
- 1 cup flaked coconut
- 1 cup chopped pecans
- 4 eggs, beaten
- 2½ cups milk
- 2½ cups granulated sugar
- 2 cups half-and-half *or* light cream
- 2 tablespoons vanilla
- 1 teaspoon ground cinnamon
- 1 teaspoon ground nutmeg
- ⅓ cup butter *or* margarine, cut into small pieces

❖ ❖ ❖

__Cooking New Orleans Style__ is a wonderful book filled with sights, culture and tastes. The successful cookbook features typical New Orleans food alongside photographs of local scenes.

__Cooking New Orleans Style__
The Women of All Saints'
Episcopal Church
New Orleans
LOUISIANA

1 To make the Custard Sauce: In a heavy medium saucepan, stir together the 4 eggs, 1½ cups milk and ⅔ cup granulated sugar. Cook, stirring constantly, over medium heat until the egg mixture just coats a metal spoon.

2 Remove the saucepan from heat and stir in the 1 teaspoon vanilla. Quickly cool the custard by placing the saucepan in a bowl of ice water for 1 to 2 minutes, stirring constantly. (Be careful not to get any water in the sauce.) Pour the cooled custard into a bowl and cover the surface with plastic wrap. Refrigerate until ready to serve.

3 To make the Hard Sauce: In a small mixing bowl, beat the ½ cup butter or margarine and the powdered sugar with an electric mixer on medium speed for 3 to 5 minutes or until the mixture is well combined. (The mixture may still be crumbly.)

4 Beat in the 2 teaspoons vanilla and continue beating until the mixture is smooth. Cover and refrigerator to harden (about 1 hour).

5 To make the Bread Pudding: Preheat the oven to 350°. In a 3-quart rectangular baking dish layer *half* of the bread cubes, raisins, coconut and pecans. Repeat the layers; set aside.

6 In large bowl, stir together the 4 beaten eggs, 2½ cups milk, 2½ cups granulated sugar, half-and-half or light cream, 2 tablespoons vanilla, cinnamon and nutmeg.

7 Pour the milk mixture evenly over the ingredients in the baking dish. Dot with the ⅓ cup butter or margarine.

8 Bake the pudding in the 350° oven for 1 to 1¼ hours or until a knife inserted near the center comes out clean.

9 To serve: Spoon the warm Bread Pudding into serving dishes. Pass the Custard Sauce and Hard Sauce for spooning on top.

Nutrition Analysis (*Per Serving*): Calories: 690 / Cholesterol: 197 mg / Carbohydrates: 97 g / Protein: 11 g / Sodium: 318 mg / Fat: 31 g (Saturated Fat: 15 g) Potassium: 390 mg.

TRADITIONAL BREAD PUDDING

chapter three

cookies & candies

Give your tastebuds a culinary trip they'll never forget! Gazing over this vista of gastronomical goodies, you'll spot both time-honored standards such as Thumbprint Cookies and out-of-this-world innovations such as Butter Pecan Turtle Cookies. Along the way, enjoy doubly delightful Peanut Butter-Chocolate Chip Cookies, cream-filled Whoopie Pies, buttery Elephant Ears, or delicate Chocolate-Molasses Lace Cookies. And visions of Chocolate-Almond Bark or Fudge Meltaways are sure to enrapture the confection aficionados. Browse through this itinerary of munchable meccas and start planning your own voyage of baking discovery.

ULTIMATE HUNKA CHOCOLATE COOKIES

ULTIMATE HUNKA CHOCOLATE COOKIES

Makes 28 Cookies

- 2   12-ounce packages semisweet chocolate pieces
- 4   squares (4 ounces) unsweetened chocolate
- ¼   cup butter *or* margarine
- ½   cup all-purpose flour
- ½   teaspoon baking powder
- ¼   teaspoon salt
- 4   eggs
- 1⅓ cups sugar
- 2   teaspoons vanilla
- 2   cups toasted coarsely chopped walnuts, pecans *or* macadamia nuts

◆   ◆   ◆

Kay Buro was given this recipe by the mother of one of her students. Kay often made the cookies to take to school and keep in the teachers' lounge for occasional treats. Because the cookies store well, she enjoyed sharing them with friends and family at Christmas time, too. Kay suggests letting the dough rest in a cool place to help the sugar to dissolve and to give the dough a creamier texture.

Kay Buro
Our Favorite Recipes
Hope Lutheran Church
Moose Lake
MINNESOTA

1 Preheat the oven to 350°. Lightly grease a cookie sheet; set aside.

2 In a heavy saucepan over medium heat, melt *1* of the 12-ounce packages semisweet chocolate pieces, the unsweetened chocolate and butter or margarine, stirring constantly. Transfer the chocolate mixture to a large mixing bowl and let the mixture cool slightly for 10 minutes.

3 In a small bowl, stir together the flour, baking powder and salt; set aside.

4 Add the eggs, sugar and vanilla to the cooled chocolate mixture and beat with an electric mixer until well combined. Add the flour mixture and beat on low speed just until mixed. Stir in the remaining semisweet chocolate pieces and the toasted walnuts, pecans or macadamia nuts.

5 Using *¼ cup* of dough for each cookie, drop the dough 3 inches apart onto the prepared cookie sheet. Flatten each dough mound slightly.

6 Bake in the 350° oven for 12 to 15 minutes or until the edges of the cookies are firm and the surfaces are dull and cracked. Let the cookies stand for 2 minutes on the cookie sheet. Transfer the cookies to a wire rack to cool.

TIPS FROM OUR KITCHEN

To make smaller cookies: Drop the dough by rounded teaspoonfuls 2 inches apart onto lightly greased cookie sheets. Bake in a 350° oven for 8 to 10 minutes or until the edges of the cookies are firm.

These cookies tend to dry out if they are left at room temperature. Therefore, if you're planning to store these cookies for more than 2 days, place them in freezer-proof bags and freeze.

Dress-up these chocolaty cookies even more by drizzling them with a white chocolate glaze and a dark chocolate glaze. To make the white chocolate glaze: Melt 2 ounces *white confectioner's coating* with 1 teaspoon *shortening*. For the dark chocolate glaze: Melt 2 ounces *semisweet chocolate* with 1 teaspoon *shortening*.

Nutrition Analysis (*Per Cookie*): Calories: 254 / Cholesterol: 35 mg / Carbohydrates: 30 g / Protein: 4 g / Sodium: 46 mg / Fat: 16 g (Saturated Fat: 3 g) / Potassium: 144 mg.

PEANUT BUTTER-CHOCOLATE CHIP COOKIES

Makes About 4 Dozen Cookies

½	cup butter *or* margarine, softened
½	cup creamy peanut butter
½	cup granulated sugar
½	cup packed light brown sugar
2	eggs
1	teaspoon vanilla
1⅓	cups all-purpose flour
1	teaspoon baking soda
¼	teaspoon salt
1¾	cups semisweet chocolate pieces

◆　◆　◆

Marie Young McFarland collects recipes from papers, magazines and friends—basically, "from everywhere!" When she was asked to submit her favorite recipe to the Home Cookin' Mount Zion Heritage Cookbook, *she chose this recipe for Peanut Butter-Chocolate Chip Cookies "because it's a recipe my grandchildren love."*

Marie Young McFarland
Home Cookin' Mount Zion Heritage Cookbook
Mount Zion Cemetery Association
Apple Springs
TEXAS

1 Preheat the oven to 350°. Lightly grease a cookie sheet; set aside.

2 In a large mixing bowl, combine the softened butter or margarine and peanut butter. Beat with an electric mixer on medium speed until the mixture is light and fluffy. Gradually add the granulated sugar and brown sugar. Beat in the eggs and vanilla until well combined; set aside.

3 In a medium bowl, stir together the flour, baking soda and salt. Add the flour mixture and chocolate pieces to the dough. Stir until the dough is well blended.

4 Drop the batter by tablespoonfuls onto the prepared the cookie sheet. Bake in the 350° oven for 9 to 12 minutes or until the edges of the cookies are lightly browned or a slight impression remains when the cookies are lightly touched with a fingertip. Transfer the cookies to a wire rack to cool completely.

 TIPS FROM OUR KITCHEN

Don't use margarine to grease the cookie sheets; it's more likely to burn than shortening or a nonstick vegetable spray.

If you use margarine instead of butter, be sure to choose a product that's labeled "margarine," not "spread." If you use 100-percent corn oil margarine, the dough will be softer than it would be if you use other margarines.

For a peanuttier flavor, add ⅓ cup chopped peanuts to the cookie dough. Or, substitute peanut butter-flavored pieces (¾ cup) for part of the chocolate pieces.

Cool the cookie sheet between batches to keep the dough from flattening too much during baking. Light-colored cookie sheets are better than dark-colored cookie sheets; dark-colored cookie sheets can cause the cookies to overbrown on the bottoms and sides before the centers are baked.

Nutrition Analysis (*Per Cookie*): Calories: 91 / Cholesterol: 14 mg / Carbohydrates: 11 g / Protein: 2 g / Sodium: 71 mg / Fat: 5 g (Saturated Fat: 1 g) / Potassium: 51 mg.

PEANUT BUTTER-CHOCOLATE CHIP COOKIES

CHOCOLATE-MOLASSES LACE COOKIES

CHOCOLATE-MOLASSES LACE COOKIES

Makes 3 Dozen Sandwich Cookies
- ⅔ cup butter
- 2 cups quick-cooking rolled oats
- 1 cup sugar
- ⅔ cup all-purpose flour
- ¼ cup molasses
- ¼ cup milk
- 1 teaspoon vanilla
- ¼ teaspoon salt
- 1 11½-ounce package milk chocolate pieces (2 cups)

❖ ❖ ❖

Nancy Tippett told us about her former holiday baking tradition: In October, she started baking cookies, and then froze them so that she was ready to prepare her special gift trays. As a result of her advance preparation, Nancy said that often she had dozens and dozens of cookies to arrange. She also said that Chocolate Molasses Lace Cookies were her favorite—"They were the ones that attracted the attention on the cookie tray."

Nancy Tippett
<u>Angel Food</u>
The Women's Minis-tree of the
Roxborough Presbyterian Church
Philadelphia
PENNSYLVANIA

1 Preheat the oven to 375°. Line baking sheets with foil. Set aside.

2 In a medium saucepan, melt the butter. Stir in the rolled oats, sugar, flour, molasses, milk, vanilla and salt.

3 Drop by rounded teaspoonfuls 3 inches apart onto the prepared baking sheets. With floured fingertips, press down until the dough is very thin.

4 Bake in the 375° oven for 5 to 7 minutes or until the cookies are lacy and golden. Cool completely, about 15 minutes. Peel the foil away from the cookies.

5 In a medium saucepan, melt the chocolate pieces over low heat, stirring constantly. Spread about *1 teaspoon* of the melted chocolate on the bottoms of *half* of the cookies. Top with the unfrosted cookies.

 TIPS FROM OUR KITCHEN

We recommend butter for this recipe because margarines vary in amounts of water and may cause the cookies to spread too thin.

About half a package (1 cup) of chocolate pieces is enough to sandwich the cookies together. To melt the chocolate in a microwave, place the pieces in a microwave-safe container and micro-cook on 100% (high) power for 1 minute, stirring once.

Instead of creating cookie "sandwiches," you can spread the melted chocolate on top of all of the cookies.

Instead of milk chocolate, try white chocolate, such as Alpine white bars, as filling for the cookie sandwiches.

Nutrition Analysis (*Per Cookie*): Calories: 129 / Cholesterol: 11 mg / Carbohydrates: 17 g / Protein: 2 g / Sodium: 60 mg / Fat: 6 g (Saturated Fat: 2 g) / Potassium: 72 mg.

WHOOPIE PIES

Makes About 3 Dozen Whoopie Pies
Cookies:
2	cups all-purpose flour
1	cup granulated sugar
½	cup unsweetened cocoa powder
1	teaspoon baking soda
½	teaspoon baking powder
¼	teaspoon salt
½	cup sour milk
½	cup water
½	cup shortening
1	egg
1	egg yolk

Filling:
½	cup shortening
2	tablespoons all-purpose flour
1	tablespoon granulated sugar
2	teaspoons vanilla
2½	cups powdered sugar
3	tablespoons milk

◆ ◆ ◆

In a small community of about 500, the sales of the Harrington Homemakers's _Harrington Cooks_ is quite impressive—over 850 copies. According to Chairman Linda Wagner, many cookbook owners say, "this is the only cookbook I use." Profits were targeted for Harrington School projects, park beautification and community needs.

Harrington Cooks
Harrington Homemakers
Harrington
WASHINGTON

1 Preheat the oven to 400°.

2 To make the cookies: In a medium mixing bowl, combine the 2 cups flour, the 1 cup granulated sugar, the cocoa powder, baking soda, baking powder, and salt. Add the sour milk, water and the ½ cup shortening. Beat with an electric mixer on low speed until combined.

3 Beat on medium speed for 2 minutes more. Add the whole egg and egg yolk; beat for 2 minutes more.

4 Drop the dough by rounded teaspoonfuls 2 inches apart onto an ungreased cookie sheet. Bake in the 400° oven about 6 minutes or until the top springs back when lightly touched in the center. Remove the cookies from the oven and transfer them to a wire rack to cool.

5 Meanwhile, to make the filling: In a small mixing bowl, combine the ½ cup shortening, the 2 tablespoons flour, the 1 tablespoon granulated sugar and the vanilla. Beat with an electric mixer on medium speed for 30 seconds.

6 Slowly add *1¼ cups* of the powdered sugar; beat well. Add the milk. Gradually add the remaining powdered sugar; beat well.

7 Spoon about *2 teaspoons* of the filling onto *half* of the cookies. Top with the remaining cookies and sandwich together.

 TIPS FROM OUR KITCHEN

To make a surprise filling, add ½ cup miniature chocolate pieces to the filling.

To make sour milk: Pour 1½ teaspoons *lemon juice* or *white vinegar* into a 1-cup glass measure. Add enough *milk* to make ½ cup. Let the mixture stand for 5 minutes before adding it to the remainder of the ingredients.

Nutrition Analysis (*Per Pie*): Calories: 136 / Cholesterol: 12 mg / Carbohydrates: 19 g / Protein: 1 g / Sodium: 53 mg / Fat: 6 g (Saturated Fat: 2 g) / Potassium: 17 mg.

WHOOPIE PIES

ACORN COOKIES

ACORN COOKIES

Makes 48 to 60 Cookies

1	cup butter *or* margarine, melted
¾	cup packed light brown sugar
1¾	cups finely chopped pecans
1	teaspoon vanilla
2¾	cups all-purpose flour
½	teaspoon baking powder
1	cup (6 ounces) semisweet chocolate pieces

◆　　◆　　◆

A love of theater can quickly become an all-absorbing passion and the members of the Backers Volunteer Board of the Repertory Theater of St. Louis provide us with no exception to this rule. The energetic group supports their theater in every imaginable way, from making costumes to appearing on stage as extras. They created Cooking for Applause to be a recipe source for catered parties given for new subscribers and to raise money for the theater. Of course, Jacqui Thompson's Acorn Cookies are always in demand.

Jacqui Thompson
Cooking for Applause
Backers Volunteer Board
St. Louis
MISSOURI

1 Preheat oven to 325°.

2 In a large mixing bowl, beat the butter or margarine with the brown sugar until well blended. Stir in *¾ cup* of the pecans and the vanilla.

3 In a medium bowl, stir together the flour and baking powder. Beat the flour mixture into the butter mixture until combined.

4 Roll pieces of the dough into small (1-inch-diameter) balls. Place the balls 1 inch apart on ungreased cookie sheets.

5 To shape the cookies, gently press down on each cookie to flatten the bottom, then pinch up the top of the cookie to form the point of the acorn.

6 Bake the cookies for 12 to 15 minutes or until they are golden. Cool the cookies on wire racks.

7 Melt the chocolate in the top of a double boiler over warm water.

8 Dip the flattened bottoms of the cookies into the chocolate to make a "cap" for the acorn, then dip the chocolate cap into the remaining chopped pecans. Cool the cookies completely on waxed paper.

 TIPS FROM OUR KITCHEN

These cookies are so easy you don't even need a mixing bowl. You can mix them right in the saucepan you use to melt the butter.

If you don't own a double boiler, just melt the chocolate in a heavy saucepan over very low heat and watch it carefully. Or to melt the chocolate in your microwave: Place the chocolate pieces in a 2-cup glass measure. Cook the chocolate uncovered, on 100% power (high), for 1½ to 2½ minutes or until it is soft enough to stir smooth, stirring every minute of cooking.

Nutrition Analysis *(Per Cookie):* Calories: 122 / Cholesterol: 10 mg / Carbohydrates: 13 g / Protein: 1 g / Sodium: 47 mg / Fat: 8 g (Saturated Fat: 3 g) / Potassium: 63 mg.

VON TRAPP RUM PENNIES

Makes 6 to 7 Dozen Cookies

Cookies:
- 2 egg whites
- 2 cups sifted powdered sugar
- 1 cup ground pecans
- 1 cup ground walnuts
- ½ teaspoon dark rum

Icing:
- ⅔ cup sifted powdered sugar
- 2 to 3 teaspoons dark rum

✦ ✦ ✦

When we contacted Emilie de Brigard to talk about her recipe for Von Trapp Rum Pennies, we learned that its original name was Von Trapp Rum Stangerln. "Stangerln" is Austrian dialect for "small stick." Emilie was given this recipe by her aunt, Mrs. Julius Meier. These little cookies are a very important part of Mrs. Meier's Christmas repertoire and though Mrs. Meier is in her eighties, she still makes her Stangerln every year.

Emilie de Brigard
Connecticut À La Carte
The Junior League of Hartford
West Hartford
CONNECTICUT

1 Preheat oven to 350°. Line cookie sheets with aluminum foil, parchment paper or plain brown paper. If using foil, lightly grease. Set aside.

2 To make the cookies: In a large mixing bowl, beat the egg whites with an electric mixer on medium speed until stiff peaks form (tips stand straight). Fold in the powdered sugar and the pecans and walnuts. Stir in the rum.

3 Drop the batter by teaspoons onto the lined cookie sheets approximately 2 inches apart.

4 Bake in the 350° oven about 10 minutes or until the cookies are dry and the edges are lightly browned. Cool the cookies completely on the cookie sheets.

5 Once the cookies are cool, carefully peel them off the foil or paper.

6 To make the icing: In a small mixing bowl, stir together the powdered sugar and enough rum to make a thin consistency. Spoon the icing over the cookies.

7 To store, place the cookies in an airtight container.

TIPS FROM OUR KITCHEN

To make sure your beaten egg whites are as fluffy as they can be, let the egg whites stand at room temperature for 30 minutes before beating.

Nutrition Analysis *(Per Cookie)*: Calories: 36 / Cholesterol: 0 mg / Carbohydrates: 4 g / Protein: 1 g / Sodium: 2 mg / Fat: 2 g (Saturated Fat: 0 g) / Potassium: 16 mg.

VON TRAPP RUM PENNIES

THUMBPRINT COOKIES

THUMBPRINT COOKIES

Makes 30 Cookies
¼ cup butter *or* margarine, softened
¼ cup shortening
¼ cup packed brown sugar
1 egg yolk
½ teaspoon vanilla
1 cup all-purpose flour
1 egg white
¾ cup finely chopped nuts
Jelly *or* jam of your choice

◆　　◆　　◆

Joyce Bowman's daughter gave her this recipe for Thumbprint Cookies. Joyce told us that her daughter used this recipe in a middle school cooking class well over 20 years ago. Although Joyce doesn't bake as often as she once did, she remembers that Thumbprint Cookies were something fun for children to make.

Joyce Bowman
Under the Willows
San Jose Auxiliary to the Lucile Salter Packard Children's Hospital at Stanford
San Jose
CALIFORNIA

1 In a medium mixing bowl, combine the softened butter or margarine, shortening, brown sugar, egg yolk and vanilla. Beat the mixture with an electric mixer on medium speed until well blended. Beat in the flour until the dough holds together.

2 Preheat the oven to 350°. Shape the dough by teaspoonfuls into 1-inch balls. Slightly beat the egg white. Dip *each* dough ball into the beaten egg white; roll each ball and spoon the nuts over to coat. Place the coated dough balls 1 inch apart on ungreased cookie sheets.

3 Carefully press your thumb in the center of *each* dough ball to make a deep impression.

4 Bake in the 350° oven about 10 minutes or until the cookies are lightly browned. Immediately transfer the cookies to a wire rack; cool completely.

5 Using a teaspoon, fill each cookie thumbprint with the jelly or jam of your choice.

 TIPS FROM OUR KITCHEN

Walnuts or pecans often are used for this recipe, but you can also use cashews, hazelnuts or macadamia nuts.

You'll need about ⅓ cup of jelly or jam to fill all of the cookies in this recipe. Or, if desired, fill the thumbprints with a powdered sugar frosting. You can use food coloring to tint the frosting, too.

To make Chocolate Thumbprint Cookies: Substitute ½ cup *granulated sugar* for the ¼ cup brown sugar and add 1 ounce (1 square) melted and cooled *unsweetened chocolate* with the vanilla. Bake the cookies in the 350° oven about 10 minutes or until the edges are set.

Nutrition Analysis (*Per Cookie*): Calories: 89 / Cholesterol: 11 mg / Carbohydrates: 10 g / Protein: 1 g / Sodium: 20 mg / Fat: 5 g (Saturated Fat: 2 g) / Potassium: 33 mg.

RICOTTA COOKIES

Makes 5½ Dozen Cookies

Cookies:

2	cups granulated sugar
1	cup margarine *or* butter, softened
3	eggs
2	teaspoons vanilla
4	cups all-purpose flour
1	teaspoon baking soda
1	teaspoon salt
1	15-ounce carton ricotta cheese (2 cups)

Frosting:

1	3-ounce package cream cheese, softened
½	cup margarine *or* butter
1	teaspoon vanilla
1	cup sifted powdered sugar
	Ground nutmeg (optional)

◆　◆　◆

The Easter Seal of Approval Cookbook is the result of the efforts of parents, relatives, staff, volunteers and friends of the Easter Seal Society Parents Auxiliary of the Bucks County Center. Profits from sales have been used to help provide services to the preschoolers, campers and outpatients who use the Bucks County Center.

Judy Manchester
Easter Seal of Approval Cookbook
Easter Seal Society
Levittown
PENNSYLVANIA

1 Preheat the oven to 350°.

2 To make the cookies: In a large mixing bowl, beat the granulated sugar and the 1 cup margarine or butter with an electric mixer on medium to high speed until combined.

3 Add the eggs and the 2 teaspoons vanilla; beat until creamy. Add *half* of the flour, the baking soda and salt; beat until well blended. Stir in the remaining flour and the ricotta cheese.

4 Drop the dough by rounded tablespoons, 2 inches apart, onto an ungreased cookie sheet.

5 Bake in the 350° oven about 12 minutes or until the bottoms of the cookies are browned. The cookie tops *should not brown.* Transfer the cookies to wire racks to cool.

6 To make the frosting: Beat together the cream cheese, the ½ cup margarine or butter and the 1 teaspoon vanilla until light and fluffy. Gradually add the powdered sugar; mix well. Spread the frosting on the cooled cookies. If desired, sprinkle with ground nutmeg. Store the frosted cookies, covered, in the refrigerator.

TIPS FROM OUR KITCHEN

Unless you have refrigerator space for several plates of single-layered, frosted cookies, refrigerate the cookies unfrosted and frost them just before serving. Store the unused frosting in a covered container in the refrigerator. For freezer storage, freeze the frosted cookies in a single layer, then package them in layered stacks, if desired. Separate the layers immediately after removing the cookies from the freezer and thaw the cookies in a single layer.

Ricotta cheese is a fresh, moist, white cheese with a very mild, semisweet flavor and a soft, slightly grainy texture. It is made from whey—the thin, watery liquid formed when milk is coagulated to make other cheeses. Whole or skim milk is sometimes added.

Making cookies of equal size requires scooping equal amounts of dough. Use a rounded tablespoonful for each one.

Nutrition Analysis (*Per Cookie*): Calories: 109 / Cholesterol: 13 mg / Carbohydrates: 13 g / Protein: 2 g / Sodium: 110 mg / Fat: 5 g (Saturated Fat: 1 g) / Potassium: 22 mg.

RICOTTA COOKIES

ELEPHANT EARS

ELEPHANT EARS

Makes 18 Cookies

1	package active dry yeast
¼	cup warm water (105° to 115°)
2	cups all-purpose flour
4½	teaspoons sugar
½	teaspoon salt
½	cup butter *or* margarine
½	cup milk, scalded and cooled to lukewarm
1	egg yolk
2	tablespoons butter *or* margarine, melted
1½	cups sugar
1	tablespoon ground cinnamon
1 to 1½	cups chopped pecans *or* walnuts

❖   ❖   ❖

Mary Robert has a fond memory from her youth of her father buying Elephant Ears at the bakery. When the time came to submit recipes to the St. Paul's Episcopal Church cookbook, she and Freda McDonald found a recipe and made changes to create their version of Elephant Ears.

**Mary Robert and
Freda McDonald**
<u>**Loaves and Fishes from the
Eastern Shore**</u>
**The Episcopal Churchwomen
St. Paul's Episcopal Church
Fairhope
ALABAMA**

1 Dissolve the yeast in the warm water. Let the mixture stand for 5 minutes.

2 In a large mixing bowl, stir together the flour, the 4½ teaspoons sugar and salt. Using a pastry blender, cut in the ½ cup butter or margarine until the mixture resembles coarse crumbs.

3 Stir together the scalded milk and egg yolk. Stir in the yeast mixture. Add the milk mixture to the flour mixture, mixing well. Cover the bowl and refrigerate for 2 hours.

4 Turn the mixture out onto a lightly floured surface. Roll the dough into an 18x10-inch rectangle. Brush with the 2 tablespoons melted butter or margarine.

5 In a small bowl, stir together the 1½ cups sugar and the cinnamon. Sprinkle *½ cup* of the cinnamon-sugar mixture over the dough. Roll the dough, jelly roll fashion, starting with a long side. Pinch along the long edges (do not seal). Place the roll, seam side down and slice it into eighteen 1-inch-wide slices.

6 Preheat the oven to 400°.

7 Lightly sprinkle a portion of the remaining cinnamon-sugar mixture

over a piece of waxed paper placed on your work surface. Onto this, place a slice of the cookie dough and roll the slice out to an oblong shape (elephant ear) about ⅛-inch thick, turning it over once. (These cookies will look more like "elephant ears" if you only roll forward and back, instead of rolling outward in all directions from the center of the dough.)

8 Carefully transfer the rolled slice to an ungreased cookie sheet by inverting it onto the cookie sheet and peeling away the waxed paper. Repeat with the remaining slices, sprinkling the waxed paper with additional cinnamon-sugar mixture each time.

9 Sprinkle the rolled slices with the remaining cinnamon-sugar mixture and the pecans or walnuts. With your fingers, lightly press the nuts into dough.

10 Bake the cookies in the 400° oven for 10 to 12 minutes or until lightly browned. Using a spatula, carefully remove the cookies from the cookie sheet and transfer them to wire racks to cool.

 TIPS FROM OUR KITCHEN

"Scalded" milk means it has been heated to just below boiling when tiny bubbles just begin to appear around the edge of the milk.

Nutrition Analysis (*Per Cookie*): Calories: 215 / Cholesterol: 30 mg / Carbohydrates: 29 g / Protein: 2 g / Sodium: 129 mg / Fat: 11 g (Saturated Fat: 4 g) / Potassium: 60 mg.

SOFT GINGER COOKIES

Makes 7 Dozen 2½- to 3-inch Cookies

1	cup butter *or* margarine
1	cup sugar
1	egg
1	cup molasses
1	cup sour milk *or* buttermilk
2	teaspoons baking soda
1	teaspoon ground cinnamon
1	teaspoon ground ginger
½	teaspoon salt
¼	teaspoon ground cloves
¼	teaspoon ground allspice
¼	teaspoon ground nutmeg
7	cups all-purpose flour

❖   ❖   ❖

Pearl Tabor Jones tells us that she made her Soft Ginger Cookies for over fifty years. Pearl always made them using a snowman cookie cutter—children told her that the cookies didn't taste the same unless they were made in the shape of a snowman! At Christmas, she would wrap each cookie individually and close the packages with a Christmas seal.

Pearl Tabor Jones
Grandmother's Recipes
For The Modern Cook
Havenwood-Heritage Heights
Concord
NEW HAMPSHIRE

1 Preheat the oven to 375°.

2 In a very large mixing bowl, beat the butter or margarine with an electric mixer on medium speed for 30 seconds. Add the sugar and beat until thoroughly combined. Then add the egg and beat well.

3 Add the molasses, then the sour milk. Stir in the baking soda, cinnamon, ginger, salt, cloves, allspice and nutmeg. Gradually stir in the flour. Divide the dough into *thirds* and wrap *each* piece in plastic wrap; chill thoroughly.

4 On a lightly floured surface, roll *one-third* of the dough at a time to ⅛-inch thickness. Cut the dough into desired shapes using cookie cutters.

5 Bake the cookies on an ungreased cookie sheet in the 375° oven for 6 to 8 minutes or until the edges are set. Cool the cookies on a wire rack. Repeat with the remaining dough.

 TIPS FROM OUR KITCHEN

To make 1 cup sour milk, measure 1 tablespoon lemon juice or vinegar into a 1-cup glass measure. Add enough milk to equal 1 cup and let it stand 5 minutes before adding it to the recipe.

Either dark or light molasses can be used in this recipe. Dark molasses is less sweet and gives a darker color and a more distinct molasses flavor than the milder flavored light molasses.

The two-part secret for success with cut-out cookies is making sure the dough is well chilled and rolling the dough out on a floured surface. Use one-third of the dough at a time and leave the remainder refrigerated. Using a floured pastry cloth and cloth-covered rolling pin helps to reduce dough-sticking problems.

Measuring the dough thickness with a ruler makes it easier to cut cookies that will bake evenly. If you want to bake both large and small cookies, group equal-sized cookies on separate cookie sheets so that all of the cookies on the same cookie sheet will be done at the same time.

Nutrition Analysis (*Per Cookie*): Calories: 75 / Cholesterol: 9 mg / Carbohydrates: 12 g / Protein: 1 g / Sodium: 58 g / Fat: 2 g (Saturated Fat: 1 g) / Potassium: 52 mg.

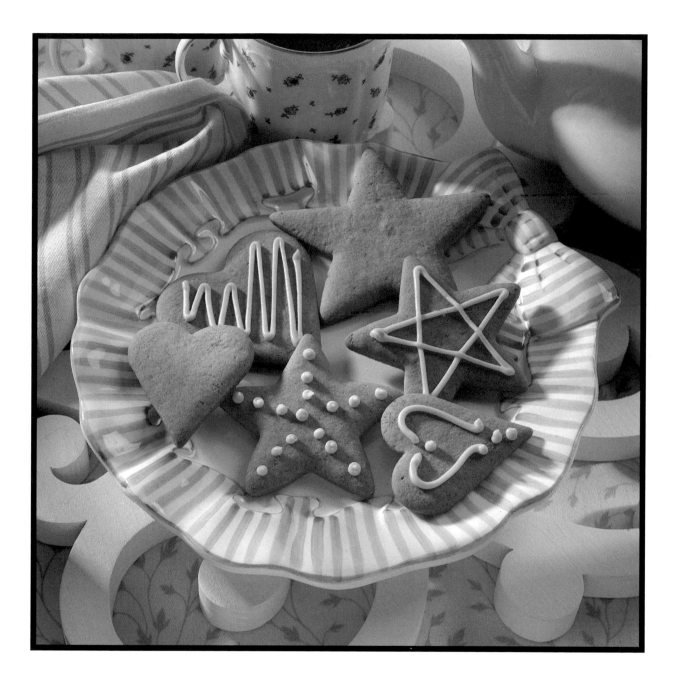

SOFT GINGER COOKIES

BROWN SUGARS

BROWN SUGARS

Makes 2 to 3½ Dozen Cookies
½ cup butter *or* margarine
½ cup packed dark brown sugar
½ cup granulated sugar
1 egg
1 teaspoon vanilla
2 cups all-purpose flour
½ teaspoon baking soda
⅛ teaspoon salt
½ cup ground walnuts
Granulated sugar

♦ ♦ ♦

Jo-Anne Brown loves to bake and cook, and this recipe for Brown Sugars is her favorite. A neighbor gave her the recipe in 1955, and Jo-Anne said that she has made these cookies once a week for the past twenty-five years. All of her children use this recipe, and they eventually will pass it along to their children. Jo-Anne recommends that you use toasted pecans instead of walnuts "for a richer taste." She also suggested serving the cookies at birthday parties topped with ice cream.

Jo-Anne Brown
Mark Twain Library Cookbook
The Mark Twain Library
Association
Redding
CONNECTICUT

1 Preheat the oven to 350°. Lightly grease a cookie sheet; set aside.

2 In a large mixing bowl, cream the butter or margarine with an electric mixer on medium speed. Add the brown sugar and the ½ cup granulated sugar; beat until well blended. Beat in the egg and vanilla.

3 In a medium bowl, stir together the flour, baking soda and salt. Gradually add the flour mixture to the butter mixture, beating on low speed just until combined. Add the ground walnuts; stir well.

4 Roll the dough into small balls (about 1-inch diameter). Roll the balls in the additional granulated sugar to coat. Place the sugar-coated balls 3 inches apart on the prepared cookie sheet.

5 Using a flat-bottomed glass, flatten each dough ball on the cookie sheet.

6 Bake in the 350° oven for 10 to 12 minutes or until the cookies are golden on the bottom. Transfer the cookies to wire racks to cool.

 TIPS FROM OUR KITCHEN

As always, the number of cookies made from one batch of dough will depend on their sizes. If you start with 1½-inch balls of dough and flatten them to 2 inches, you'll get about 2 dozen 2½-inch cookies. If you start with 1-inch balls and flatten them to 1½ inches, you'll get about 3½ dozen 2-inch cookies.

If you use a portable mixer, you'll want to stir in the last portion of the flour and nuts by hand.

For the best results when baking the cookies, place the cookie sheet on the middle rack of the 350° oven.

Nutrition Analysis (*Per Cookie*): Calories: 126 / Cholesterol: 19 mg / Carbohydrates: 18 g / Protein: 2 g / Sodium: 71 mg / Fat: 6 g (Saturated Fat: 3 g) / Potassium: 36 mg.

OAT AND BANANA COOKIES

Makes 4 Dozen Cookies

1½	cups all-purpose flour
1	cup sugar
1	teaspoon baking powder
1	teaspoon ground cinnamon
½	teaspoon ground nutmeg
½	teaspoon salt
½	teaspoon baking soda
⅔	cup shortening
2	eggs
1	cup mashed ripe bananas (2 *or* 3)
1½	cups rolled oats

❖   ❖   ❖

Monica Chabeste acquired her recipe for Oat and Banana Cookies (Galletas de Avena y Plantano) over forty years ago. Monica's daughter, who translated the recipe from Spanish into English, remembers eating these cookies from "way back." Monica makes the cookies on special occasions, especially Christmas, and gives them to her neighbors and friends as holiday gifts.

Mrs. Monica Chabeste
Bless This Food
Catholic Daughters Sts. Peter and Paul Catholic Church
New Braunfels
TEXAS

1 Preheat the oven to 375°. Grease the cookie sheets. Set aside.

2 In a large mixing bowl, stir together the flour, sugar, baking powder, cinnamon, nutmeg, salt and baking soda. Add the shortening, eggs and *half* of the mashed bananas. Beat about 2 minutes or until creamy with an electric mixer on low speed.

3 Add the remaining mashed bananas and oats; stir well. Drop by teaspoonfuls onto the prepared cookie sheets.

4 Bake in the 375° oven about 10 minutes or until lightly browned. Using a spatula, transfer the cookies from the cookie sheets to a wire rack to cool.

 TIPS FROM OUR KITCHEN

To make uniformly sized cookies, use the same amount of dough for each one. To make them the same shape, round a teaspoonful or soup spoonful of the dough against the side of the mixing bowl.

To maintain the freshness of these cookies, store them in a tightly covered container at room temperature. Or, for longer storage, place the container in the freezer.

The rolled oats add a nut-like flavor to these cookies. If you prefer a nuttier flavor, toast the oats first. Spread the oats in a shallow baking pan and bake in a 350° oven for 15 to 20 minutes or until lightly browned, stirring occasionally. Cool.

For a variation, add 1 cup raisins or chopped dates to the dough. You might also frost the cookies with a powdered sugar glaze.

Nutrition Analysis *(Per Cookie)*: Calories: 71 / Cholesterol: 9 mg / Carbohydrates: 10 g / Protein: 1 g / Sodium: 40 mg / Fat: 3 g (Saturated Fat: 1 g) / Potassium: 34 mg.

OAT AND BANANA COOKIES

SNOBALL COOKIES

SNOBALL COOKIES

Makes 5 Dozen Cookies
1½ cups ground walnuts
1 cup margarine *or* butter, softened
½ cup sifted powdered sugar
2 teaspoons vanilla
2¼ cups all-purpose flour
Sifted powdered sugar

◆ ◆ ◆

Orcas Island is the largest island in the San Juan Islands, located between the state of Washington, and Vancouver Island, British Columbia. The island's population normally is 3,500, although it doubles during the summer months. Residents include "(apart from fine cooks) poets and painters, writers and thinkers…" It is an area rich in culture, and much of that culture is presented in Orcas Cuisine through recipes, sketches and the preface written by a local writer.

Edith Vestey
Orcas Cuisine
Orcas Island Medical Guild
Eastsound
Orcas Island
WASHINGTON

1 Preheat the oven to 400°.

2 In a large mixing bowl using an electric mixer, combine the ground walnuts, softened margarine or butter and the ½ cup powdered sugar until the mixture is fluffy. Mix in the vanilla. Add the flour; beat until the mixture is well blended.

3 Roll teaspoonfuls of the cookie dough into 1-inch balls. Place the dough balls 2 inches apart on ungreased cookie sheets. Bake in the 400° oven for 8 to 10 minutes or until the cookies are set, but not browned.

4 Place the additional powdered sugar on a piece of waxed paper or in a shallow bowl or pie plate. While the cookies are still warm, roll them in the powdered sugar until they are coated. Place the coated cookies on a wire rack to cool completely. When the cookies are cool, roll them in the powdered sugar again.

 TIPS FROM OUR KITCHEN

If desired, toast the nuts before grinding them to bring out their full flavor. To toast: Place the nuts in a small skillet and cook over medium heat for 5 to 10 minutes or until the nuts are golden, stirring often. Or, spread the nuts in a thin layer in a shallow baking pan. Bake in a 350° oven for 5 to 10 minutes or until toasted, stirring once or twice.

Use a food processor or nut grinder to grind the walnuts.

You can substitute pecans, hazelnuts or macadamia nuts for the walnuts in this recipe.

Be sure to use 1 rounded teaspoonful for each cookie. Even though perfectly shaped balls aren't necessary, the yield and baking time depend upon the cookies being very similar in size.

Instead of rolling each warm cookie in powdered sugar, you can place them in a plastic bag with the additional powdered sugar and gently shake to coat the cookies.

Nutrition Analysis (*Per Cookie*): Calories: 62 / Cholesterol: 0 mg / Carbohydrates: 5 g / Protein: 1 g / Sodium: 36 mg / Fat: 4 g (Saturated Fat: 1 g) / Potassium: 17 mg.

Neapolitan Cookies

Makes 72 to 84 Cookies

2½ cups all-purpose flour
1½ teaspoons baking powder
½   teaspoon salt
1   cup margarine *or* butter
1½ cups sugar
1   egg
1   teaspoon vanilla
½   teaspoon almond extract
5   drops red food coloring
½   cup finely chopped walnuts
1   ounce unsweetened
    chocolate, melted and
    cooled to room
    temperature

◆   ◆   ◆

Lovely to look at, delightful to eat! This three-layer cookie really stands out in a crowd. Just ask Eve Rogers. She says this recipe is simple and different, a variation of an old Italian favorite—an eye-catcher without the fuss. Whether she brings them to Christmas parties, bridge club or high school bake sales, Eve assures us that they are always a success. (If you're making these for small children, she suggests leaving out the nuts.)

Eve Rogers
Three Rivers Cookbook
Child Health of Sewickley, Inc.
Sewickley
PENNSYLVANIA

1 Line a 9x5x3-inch loaf pan with waxed paper, allowing the ends of the paper to hang over the sides of the pan.

2 In a small bowl, stir together the flour, baking powder and salt.

3 In a medium mixing bowl, beat the margarine or butter with an electric mixer on medium speed for 30 seconds. Add the sugar and beat until the mixture is fluffy. Add the egg and vanilla, and beat just until the ingredients are combined. Slowly add the flour mixture, beating on medium speed about 3 minutes or until all the ingredients are combined.

4 Divide the dough into 3 portions and place each in a separate bowl. Stir the almond extract and red food coloring into 1 dough portion. Stir the chopped walnuts into the second portion and the melted chocolate into the remaining portion.

5 Pat the pink dough evenly into the bottom of the prepared loaf pan. Pat the dough with nuts over the pink dough. Top with the chocolate dough. Cover the pan and chill in the refrigerator at least 4 hours or until the dough is firm enough to slice.

6 Preheat oven to 350°. Remove the chilled dough from the pan by lifting the waxed paper ends; remove the waxed paper.

7 Using a sharp knife, cut the block of cookie dough lengthwise in half. Cut each cookie block crosswise into ⅛- to ¼-inch-wide slices. Arrange the slices about 1 inch apart on ungreased cookie sheets.

8 Bake in the 350° oven for 10 to 12 minutes or until the edges are firm and light brown. Cool the cookies on the sheet for 1 minute, then transfer to a wire rack to cool completely.

 Tips from Our Kitchen

If you wish, bake half the batch and freeze the other. Then thaw the frozen dough in the refrigerator and bake as directed.

Nutrition Analysis (*Per Cookie*): Calories: 60 / Cholesterol: 3 mg / Carbohydrates: 7 g / Protein: 1 g / Sodium: 52 mg / Fat: 3 g (Saturated Fat: 1g) / Potassium: 14mg.

NEAPOLITAN COOKIES

RUBY DATE BARS

RUBY DATE BARS

Makes 36 Bars

3 cups fresh *or* frozen cranberries

1 8-ounce package chopped, pitted dates

1½ cups water

¾ cup sugar

2 teaspoons finely shredded lemon peel

1 tablespoon lemon juice

1 cup packed light brown sugar

½ cup margarine *or* butter, softened

¼ cup shortening

½ teaspoon salt

½ teaspoon baking soda

½ teaspoon ground cinnamon

1½ cups all-purpose flour

1¼ cups quick-cooking oats

◆   ◆   ◆

The Women of Central Presbyterian Church put together the cookbook Central Cuisine *to celebrate the 135th Anniversary of the founding of the church. The building was constructed in 1889, and is included in the National Register of Historic Places. Proceeds from cookbook sales help fund needed renovations.*

Ardietta McClellan
Central Cuisine
Central Presbyterian Church
Saint Paul
MINNESOTA

1 In a large saucepan, combine the cranberries, dates, water, granulated sugar, lemon peel and lemon juice.

2 Bring the cranberry-date mixture to a boil over high heat, stirring frequently. Reduce the heat and simmer, uncovered, about 12 minutes or until the mixture is thickened, stirring occasionally. Cool slightly.

3 Preheat oven to 375°. Grease a 13x9x2-inch baking pan.

4 In a large mixing bowl, combine the brown sugar, margarine or butter, and shortening. Beat with an electric mixer until the mixture is light and fluffy. Add the salt, baking soda and cinnamon.

5 Add the flour, about ½ *cup* at a time. Once the flour is incorporated, stir in the oats (the mixture will look crumbly). Set *2 cups* of the oat mixture aside for the topping. Press the remaining oat mixture evenly into the prepared pan.

6 Evenly spread the cranberry-date mixture on top of the oat mixture in the pan. Sprinkle with the reserved oat mixture. Bake in the 375° oven for 25 to 27 minutes or until the topping is lightly browned. Cool on a wire rack. Cut into 2x1½-inch bars.

 TIPS FROM OUR KITCHEN

To make chopping whole dates easier, dip your knife in water frequently. The water will keep the dates from sticking to the knife. Or, use kitchen shears, dipping them in water between snips.

Since cranberries are seasonal, stock up on them while you can. Double wrap a bag of cranberries with freezer wrap and freeze for up to 9 months. (It is not necessary to thaw the berries before using.)

These bars will be cholesterol-free if you use vegetable shortening in place of the butter or margarine.

Nutrition Analysis *(Per Bar)*: Calories: 123 / Cholesterol: 0 mg / Carbohydrates: 21 g / Protein: 1 g / Sodium: 73 mg / Fat: 4 g (Saturated Fat: 1 g) / Potassium: 86 mg.

BUTTER PECAN TURTLE COOKIES

Makes 24 Bars

Crust:
- 2 cups all-purpose flour
- 1 cup packed brown sugar
- ½ cup unsalted *or* regular butter
- 1 cup pecan halves

Caramel Layer:
- ⅔ cup unsalted *or* regular butter
- ½ cup packed brown sugar
- 1 cup milk chocolate pieces

◆   ◆   ◆

For the past nine years, Millie Murphy has made approximately 9,000 of her Butter Pecan Turtle Cookies for the Everywoman's Resource Center's Designer's Showhouse. Millie and her sister form an assembly line and, using only two stoves, "bake for four solid weeks." Because Millie does all of the baking out of her own home, she has learned a lot of shortcuts! Millie also bakes Butter Pecan Turtle Cookies to help out with other fund-raisers in the area.

Millie Murphy
Dinner by Design
Everywoman's Resource Center
Topeka
KANSAS

1 Preheat the oven to 350°.

2 To make the crust: In a large bowl, stir together the flour and the 1 cup brown sugar. Using a pastry blender or 2 knives, cut in the ½ cup butter until the mixture resembles fine crumbs.

3 Pat the flour mixture over the bottom of an ungreased 13x9x2-inch baking pan. Sprinkle the pecan halves evenly over the unbaked crust.

4 To make the Caramel Layer: In a heavy 1-quart saucepan, stir together the ⅔ cup butter and the ½ cup brown sugar. Cook over medium-high heat, stirring constantly, until well blended and the entire surface of the mixture begins to boil. Boil the mixture for 1 minute, stirring constantly; remove from heat. Pour the caramel mixture evenly over the pecans and crust.

5 Bake in the 350° oven about 20 minutes or until the entire Caramel Layer is bubbly and the crust is a light golden brown. Remove the pan from the oven; immediately sprinkle the milk chocolate pieces over the Caramel Layer; let stand for 2 to 3 minutes. Using a knife, slightly swirl the chocolate pieces as they melt; leave some chocolate pieces

whole to create a marbled effect. *Do not spread the chocolate pieces.*

6 Let the cookies cool completely; cut into 24 bars.

 TIPS FROM OUR KITCHEN

If you want perfectly shaped bars, line the pan with aluminum foil. After the bars have cooled, use the aluminum foil to lift out the bars and then transfer them to a cutting board and cut them.

Butter easily absorbs the flavor and odor of other foods. Keep it in its original protective wrapping and wrap any left-overs in plastic wrap. Salted butter can be kept in the refrigerator up to 3 weeks and unsalted butter up to 2 weeks. Both kinds can be wrapped in freezer-safe wrap and frozen for 6 to 9 months.

Brown sugar is a processed mixture of granulated sugar and molasses. Light brown sugar has less molasses flavor than dark brown sugar. Do not substitute liquid brown sugar in recipes that specify brown sugar.

Nutrition Analysis (*Per Bar*): Calories: 232 / Cholesterol: 24 mg / Carbohydrates: 26 g / Protein: 2 g / Sodium: 14 mg / Fat: 14 g (Saturated Fat: 7 g) / Potassium: 105 mg.

BUTTER PECAN TURTLE COOKIES

DOUBLE-FUDGE CHOCOLATE CHIP BROWNIES

DOUBLE-FUDGE CHOCOLATE CHIP BROWNIES

Makes 24 Brownies

8	ounces semisweet chocolate, chopped
1	cup butter *or* margarine
4	eggs
3	cups sugar
1½	teaspoons vanilla
2	cups all-purpose flour
1	cup walnuts, broken into large pieces
1	cup semisweet chocolate pieces

◆   ◆   ◆

Since its inception in Ocean City, New Jersey, in 1976, the Sunshine Foundation has been making dreams such as Disney World or seaside vacations and meetings with celebrities come true for chronically and terminally ill children. Financial support, in part, comes from sales of Our Favorite Recipes, in which we discovered this exceptional recipe for Double-Fudge Chocolate Chip Brownies.

Kathy Ciorra Staintons
Our Favorite Recipes
The Cape-Atlantic Chapter of the
The Sunshine Foundation
Ocean City
NEW JERSEY

1 Preheat oven to 350°. Grease and flour a 13x9x2-inch baking pan.

2 Melt the chopped chocolate and butter or margarine in the top of a double boiler.

3 In a large bowl, beat the eggs and sugar. Add the melted chocolate mixture and vanilla; beat until blended. Add the flour and stir until blended. Stir in the nuts and the chocolate pieces.

4 Pour the batter into the prepared pan; spread evenly. Bake in the 350° oven for 30 minutes. (Brownies should be fudgy and moist; if overcooked, they will harden.) Remove from oven; cool completely. Cut into pieces about 2 inches square.

TIPS FROM OUR KITCHEN

If desired, the chocolate and butter can be melted in a heavy saucepan over low heat instead of in the top of a double boiler.

These brownies are even better the second day when they become a little firmer and are easier to cut.

Nutrition Analysis (*Per Brownie*): Calories: 316 / Cholesterol: 56 mg / Carbohydrates: 43 g / Protein: 4 g / Sodium: 95 mg / Fat: 16 g (Saturated Fat: 5 g) / Potassium: 123 mg.

GRASSHOPPER BARS

Makes 36 Bars

Brownies:
- 4 squares (4 ounces) unsweetened chocolate, melted and cooled
- 1 cup margarine *or* butter, softened
- 2 cups granulated sugar
- 4 eggs
- 2 teaspoons vanilla
- 1 cup all-purpose flour
- 1 cup chopped walnuts *or* pecans

Mint Layer:
- 4 tablespoons margarine *or* butter, softened
- 2 cups sifted powdered sugar
- 1 teaspoon peppermint flavoring
- 4 drops green food coloring
- 1 to 2 tablespoons milk

Topping:
- ⅔ cup semisweet chocolate pieces
- 6 tablespoons margarine *or* butter
- 2 teaspoons vanilla

♦   ♦   ♦

Carna Sinkula once made Grass-hopper Bars for the Church Lenten Services and she received so many compliments that she decided to submit this recipe to the church's cookbook.

Carna Sinkula
<u>*Messiah Lutheran Cookbook*</u>
The Messiah Lutheran Church
Lakeville
MINNESOTA

1 Preheat the oven to 350°. Grease and flour a 13x9x2-inch baking pan; set aside.

2 To make the Brownies: In a large mixing bowl, beat together the melted unsweetened chocolate, the 1 cup soft-ened margarine or butter, the granulated sugar, eggs and the 2 teaspoons vanilla with an electric mixer until combined. Stir in the flour and walnuts or pecans.

3 Spread the brownie batter in the prepared baking pan. Bake in the 350° oven for 25 to 30 minutes or until the center is set. Cool the Brownies in the pan on a wire rack.

4 Meanwhile, to make the Mint Layer: In a small mixing bowl using the electric mixer, beat together the 4 tablespoons softened margarine or butter, the pow-dered sugar, peppermint flavoring and green food coloring. Add enough milk to make the mixture a spreading consistency.

5 Spread the Mint Layer over the cooled Brownies. Cover the pan with plastic wrap and refrigerate for 1 hour.

6 To make the topping: In the top of a double boiler, melt the semisweet chocolate pieces, the 6 tablespoons margarine or butter and the 2 tea-spoons vanilla, stirring frequently. Remove the double boiler top from the heat and let the topping cool slightly.

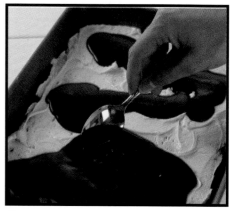

7 Carefully spread the cooled topping over the chilled Mint Layer. Let the bars stand for 1 hour; cut into 36 (2x1½-inch) bars.

 TIPS FROM OUR KITCHEN

Chilling the Brownie and Mint Layers makes it easier to spread the chocolate topping over the Mint Layer.

If you don't have a double boiler, melt the topping ingredients in a small heavy saucepan. Use low heat and stir constantly until the ingredients are combined.

These bars are good freeze-ahead treats because the chocolate topping won't discolor. Cut the cooled layers into bars and freeze them in airtight containers.

Nutrition Analysis (*Per Bar*): Calories: 209 / Cholesterol: 24 mg / Carbohydrates: 23 g / Protein: 2 g / Sodium: 105 mg / Fat: 13 g (Saturated Fat: 3 g) / Potassium: 61 mg.

GRASSHOPPER BARS

FUDGE MELTAWAYS

FUDGE MELTAWAYS

Makes 3 to 4 Dozen Bars

½	cup butter *or* margarine	
1	ounce (1 square) unsweetened chocolate	
2	cups finely crushed graham crackers (28 crackers)	
1	cup coconut	
½	cup chopped nuts	
¼	cup milk	
¼	cup granulated sugar	
1	teaspoon vanilla	
2	cups sifted powdered sugar	
¼	cup butter *or* margarine, melted	
1	tablespoon milk, light cream *or* half-and-half	
1	teaspoon vanilla	
1½	ounces (1½ squares) unsweetened chocolate	

◆　　◆　　◆

One of the fund-raisers sponsored by the San Jose Auxiliary to the Lucile Salter Packard Children's Hospital at Stanford is the Thrift Box. Organization members collect new and used clothing, household appliances and knickknacks and then sell the donated items at the Thrift Box.

Lucille Buck
Under the Willows
San Jose Auxiliary to the Lucile Salter Packard Children's Hospital at Stanford
San Jose
CALIFORNIA

1 In a medium heavy saucepan over low heat, melt the ½ cup butter or margarine and the 1 ounce chocolate, stirring occasionally. Add the crushed graham crackers, coconut, nuts, the ¼ cup milk, the granulated sugar and the 1 teaspoon vanilla. Stir until all of the ingredients are well mixed.

2 Press the crumb mixture into an ungreased 9-inch square baking pan. Cover and chill the mixture for 30 minutes to 1 hour.

3 In a small bowl, stir together the powdered sugar, the ¼ cup melted butter or margarine, the 1 tablespoon milk, light cream or half-and-half and the 1 teaspoon vanilla. Spread the butter mixture over the chilled crumb mixture; cover and chill for 1 hour.

4 In a small heavy saucepan over low heat, melt the 1½ ounces chocolate. Spread the melted chocolate over the chilled mixture in the pan.

5 Cut into bars immediately. To cut into bars: Dip a thin-bladed knife into warm *water*. First, score the top chocolate layer, then cut into bars. Cover the bars and refrigerate until serving time.

 TIPS FROM OUR KITCHEN

Use a food processor or blender to make the crumbs, or place the broken cracker squares in a heavy plastic bag and flatten them with a rolling pin.

Use your choice of nuts in this recipe, including pecans, walnuts, peanuts, macadamia nuts, almonds or hazelnuts.

To make cutting the bars and removing them from the pan easier, line the pan with aluminum foil. Then, once you've spread on the melted chocolate, carefully lift the bars from the pan using the aluminum foil, and then score the chocolate and cut into bars.

For 36 bars, make 5 cuts along each side of the pan. For 48 bars, make 5 cuts along 1 side and 7 cuts along the other. Or, for 1-inch squares to put in candy papers for a gift box, make 8 cuts along each side.

Nutrition Analysis (*Per Bar*): Calories: 113 / Cholesterol: 10 mg / Carbohydrates: 13 g / Protein: 1 g / Sodium: 66 mg / Fat: 7 g (Saturated Fat: 4 g) / Potassium: 58 mg.

CHOCOLATE-ALMOND BARK

Makes Approximately 48 Pieces
2   cups semisweet chocolate pieces
1   tablespoon shortening
½   cup raisins
½   cup chopped toasted almonds

❖   ❖   ❖

Over 3,500 copies of *A Tasteful Collection* have been sold as one of the many fund-raising efforts of the Women's Auxiliary of the Hebrew Home of Greater Washington. The cookbook presents some of the greatest recipes from cooks in the Washington area. The 2,500 Auxiliary members are dedicated to raising money to help support the home. Originally established to provide care for twelve men who had no families, the now full-care home has been in operation for more than eighty years and currently provides services for 550 residents.

A Tasteful Collection
Women's Auxiliary of the Hebrew Home of Greater Washington
Rockville
MARYLAND

1 Line a 13x9x2-inch baking pan with waxed paper or foil. Set aside.

2 In a medium saucepan, melt the chocolate and shortening over low heat until the mixture is smooth, stirring constantly. Remove from heat and stir in the raisins and *¼ cup* of the almonds.

3 Spread the chocolate mixture in the prepared pan. Sprinkle with the remaining almonds.

4 Refrigerate the bark for 30 minutes or until set. Then, break into pieces. Store in an airtight container in the refrigerator.

 TIPS FROM OUR KITCHEN

If you like, you can substitute butterscotch or peanut butter pieces or a combination of semisweet and milk chocolate pieces for the semisweet chocolate pieces in the recipe as long as the total measurement equals 2 cups.

Because the chocolate pieces soften at room temperature, you'll have to store the bark in the refrigerator until serving time.

If you wish to store the candy at room temperature, you must quick-temper the chocolate. In a 4-cup glass measure, combine the chocolate and 2 tablespoons of shortening. Pour very warm tap water (100° to 110°) into a large bowl to a depth of 1 inch. Place the

measure with the chocolate in the bowl. The water should cover the bottom half of the measure. Add more water, if necessary. (Do not splash any water into the chocolate.) Stir the chocolate constantly with a rubber spatula until melted and smooth, about 15 to 20 minutes. Do not rush. If the water in the bowl begins to cool, replace it with more warm water. Do not allow any water to touch the chocolate. Just a drop can cause the chocolate to become thick and grainy. When the chocolate is melted and smooth, it is ready to use.

Nutrition Analysis *(Per Piece)*: Calories: 48 / Cholesterol: 0 mg / Carbohydrates: 6 mg / Protein: 1 g / Sodium: 0 mg / Fat: 3 g (Saturated Fat: 0 g) / Potassium: 43 mg.

CHOCOLATE-ALMOND BARK

HELEN'S FUDGE

Makes About 5 Pounds (96 Pieces)
- 5½ cups sugar
- 1 12-ounce can evaporated milk
- 1½ cups butter *or* margarine (3 sticks)
- 6 squares (6 ounces) unsweetened chocolate, melted
- 1 12-ounce package semisweet chocolate pieces
- 1 tablespoon vanilla
- Dash salt
- 1 13-ounce jar marshmallow creme

❖　　❖　　❖

Mary Lou Norcross said that Helen's Fudge is her mother-in-law's trademark recipe. Mary Lou has had the recipe for 32 years now, and it's a favorite because it's a fast, easy, no-fail recipe. Mary Lou makes the fudge every year and tells us that although it can be stored in an airtight container for weeks in the refrigerator, it never lasts that long!

Mary Lou Norcross
<u>*Southern Elegance*</u>
Junior League of Gaston County
Gastonia
NORTH CAROLINA

1 Butter a 13x9x2-inch baking pan; set aside.

2 In a heavy 4½-quart Dutch oven, stir together the sugar, evaporated milk and butter or margarine. Cook and stir over medium heat until the mixture comes to a boil. Boil for 8 minutes, stirring constantly.

3 Remove the pan from the heat; stir in the melted unsweetened chocolate, semisweet chocolate pieces, vanilla and salt until the mixture is well blended. Stir in the marshmallow creme until no white streaks remain.

4 Pour the chocolate mixture into the prepared pan. Let the fudge sit until firm; cut it into 96 pieces, wiping the knife with a damp cloth between cuts. Store the fudge, covered, in the refrigerator.

 TIPS FROM OUR KITCHEN

You'll need a saucepan that holds more than 3 quarts of liquid to allow the sugar and milk mixture to boil without splashing over the rim of the pan.

You can melt the chocolate used in this recipe in a microwave-safe bowl. Micro-cook, uncovered, on 100% power (high) for 3 to 5 minutes or until the chocolate is soft enough to stir into a smooth mixture. Remember, the chocolate won't look melted until you stir it.

Chocolate is best stored in a tightly covered container at a temperature between 60° and 78°. Chocolate that has been stored under warm or humid conditions, however, may develop a gray color or "bloom." This doesn't hurt the quality of the chocolate, and the color will disappear when the chocolate is melted. If you refrigerate chocolate during hot weather, wrap it tightly in aluminum foil and seal the aluminum foil packets in a plastic bag; this prevents the chocolate from absorbing other food odors. Then, when bringing the chocolate to room temperature, leave it wrapped so that moisture doesn't condense and cause lumping while it melts.

Nutrition Analysis (*Per Piece*): Calories: 110 / Cholesterol: 8 mg / Carbohydrates: 18 g / Protein: 1 g / Sodium: 38 mg / Fat: 5 g (Saturated Fat: 3 g) / Potassium: 41 mg.

recipe index

Metric Cooking Hints

By making a few conversions, cooks in Australia, Canada, and the United Kingdom can use the recipes in *America's Best-Loved Community Recipes: Desserts* with confidence. The charts on this page provide a guide for converting measurements from the U.S. customary system, which is used throughout this book, to the imperial and metric systems. There also is a conversion table for oven temperatures to accommodate the differences in oven calibrations.

Volume and Weight: Americans traditionally use cup measures for liquid and solid ingredients. The chart (top right) shows the approximate imperial and metric equivalents. If you are accustomed to weighing solid ingredients, here are some helpful approximate equivalents.

■ 1 cup butter, caster sugar, or rice = 8 ounces = about 250 grams
■ 1 cup flour = 4 ounces = about 125 grams
■ 1 cup icing sugar = 5 ounces = about 150 grams
   Spoon measures are used for smaller amounts of ingredients. Although the size of the tablespoon varies slightly among countries. However, for practical purposes and for recipes in this book, a straight substitution is all that's necessary.

   Measurements made using cups or spoons should always be level, unless stated otherwise.

Product Differences: Most of the ingredients called for in the recipes in this book are available in English-speaking countries. However, some are known by different names. Here are some common American ingredients and their possible counterparts:
■ Sugar is granulated or caster sugar.
■ Powdered sugar is icing sugar.
■ All-purpose flour is plain household flour or white flour. When self-rising flour is used in place of all-purpose flour in a recipe that calls for leavening, omit the leavening agent (baking soda or baking powder) and salt.
■ Light corn syrup is golden syrup.
■ Cornstarch is cornflour.
■ Baking soda is bicarbonate of soda.
■ Vanilla is vanilla essence.

Useful Equivalents

⅛ teaspoon = 0.5ml	⅔ cup = 5 fluid ounces = 150ml
¼ teaspoon = 1ml	¾ cup = 6 fluid ounces = 175ml
½ teaspoon = 2 ml	1 cup = 8 fluid ounces = 250ml
1 teaspoon = 5 ml	2 cups = 1 pint
¼ cup = 2 fluid ounces = 50ml	2 pints = 1 litre
⅓ cup = 3 fluid ounces = 75ml	½ inch =1 centimetre
½ cup = 4 fluid ounces = 125ml	1 inch = 2 centimetres

Baking Pan Sizes

American	Metric
8x1½-inch round baking pan	20x4-centimetre sandwich or cake tin
9x1½-inch round baking pan	23x3.5-centimetre sandwich or cake tin
11x7x1½-inch baking pan	28x18x4-centimetre baking pan
13x9x2-inch baking pan	32.5x23x5-centimetre baking pan
12x7½x2-inch baking dish	30x19x5-centimetre baking pan
15x10x2-inch baking pan	38x25.5x2.5-centimetre baking pan (Swiss roll tin)
9-inch pie plate	22x4- or 23x4-centimetre pie plate
7- or 8-inch springform pan	18- or 20-centimetre springform or loose-bottom cake tin
9x5x3-inch loaf pan	23x13x6-centimetre or 2-pound narrow loaf pan or paté tin
1½-quart casserole	1.5-litre casserole
2-quart casserole	2-litre casserole

Oven Temperature Equivalents

Farenheit Setting	Celsius Setting*	Gas Setting
300°F	150°C	Gas Mark 2
325°F	160°C	Gas Mark 3
350°F	180°C	Gas Mark 4
375°F	190°C	Gas Mark 5
400°F	200°C	Gas Mark 6
425°F	220°C	Gas Mark 7
450°F	230°C	Gas Mark 8
Broil		Grill

Electric and gas ovens may be calibrated using Celsius. However, increase the Celsius setting 10 to 20 degrees when cooking above 160°C with an electric oven. For convection or forced-air ovens (gas or electric), lower the temperature setting 10°C when cooking at all heat levels.